50 FINDS FROM CUMBRIA

Objects from the Portable Antiquities Scheme

Dot Boughton

First published 2016

Amberley Publishing
The Hill, Stroud
Gloucestershire, GL5 4EP

www.amberley-books.com

ISBN 978 1 4456 5823 0 (print)
ISBN 978 1 4456 5824 7 (ebook)

British Library Cataloguing in Publication Data.
A catalogue record for this book is available from the British Library.

Typeset in 10pt on 13pt Celeste.
Typesetting by Amberley Publishing.
Printed in the UK.

Contents

Acknowledgements

I would like to thank my colleagues within the Portable Antiquities Scheme, especially Vanessa Oakden and Peter Reavill, who helped with additional images and advice. I should also like to thank my Cumbria line manager, Tim Padley (Keeper of Archaeology, Tullie House Museum & Art Gallery Trust) and the Archaeology Curator at the Dock Museum, Sabine Skae, for providing images of finds from the Furness peninsula. I would like to thank especially Will Lord (Beyond 2000 BC: Prehistoric Experiences), Jon Adkin and Mark Edmonds for letting me use their images of Langdale axe production and Pike o'Stickle. I am especially indebted to Barbara Birley and Sonya Galloway of the Vindolanda Trust, Carole and Graeme Stubbs (Corbridge), Mike Bishop (archaeologist) and Frances McIntosh (English Heritage) for their help with images of finds from Vindolanda. Many, many thanks also to Adam Parsons and Rachel Newman of Oxford Archaeology Ltd for their advice on the Cumwhitton Viking burials and for letting me use their images of some of the excavated finds. Unless otherwise stated, images are courtesy of the Portable Antiquities Scheme.

Most of all, I would like to thank the finders of archaeological artefacts in Cumbria for reporting them to us and letting us record them on the Portable Antiquities Scheme database (www.finds.org.uk/database) – without you, this book would have not been possible.

Foreword

The places in which we live and work have a long past, but one that is not always obvious in the landscape around us. This is a forgotten past. Most of us know little about the people who once lived in our communities fifty years ago, let alone 500, or even 5,000 years past. Like us, they lived, played and worked here, in this place, but we know almost nothing of them.

History books tell us about royalty, great lords and important churchmen, but most others are forgotten by time. The only evidence for many of these people is the objects that they left behind; sometimes buried on purpose, but more often lost by chance. Sometimes, through archaeological fieldwork, we can place these objects in a context that allows us to understand the past better, but nowadays excavation is mostly development-led and so only takes place when a new building, road or service pipe is being constructed.

A unique way of understanding the past is through the finds recorded through the Portable Antiquities Scheme, of which those chosen here by Dot Boughton (Finds Liaison Officer for Cumbria) are just fifty of over 7,500 from Cumbria recorded on its database (www.finds.org.uk). These finds are all discovered by the public, most by metal-detector users, searching in places archaeologists are unlikely to go or otherwise excavate. As such they provide important clues of underlying archaeology that, once recorded, help archaeologists understand our past – a past of the people, found by the people.

Some of these finds are truly magnificent, others less imposing. Yet, like pieces in a jigsaw puzzle they are often meaningless alone, but once placed together paint a picture. These finds therefore allow us to understand the story of people who once lived here, in Cumbria.

Dr Michael Lewis
Head of Portable Antiquities & Treasure
British Museum

Introduction

The British Museum's Portable Antiquities Scheme (PAS) is a project funded by the Department of Culture, Media and Sport that encourages the voluntary recording of archaeological objects found by members of the public in England and Wales. It does this through a network of Finds Liaison Officers (FLOs), based in local offices (museums or universities) across England and Wales. Every year many thousands of objects are discovered, a large number of these by metal-detector users or people out walking, beachcombing or gardening.

The local Finds Liaison Officer post for Cumbria is shared with Lancashire: since 2004 the FLO has been recording finds both at the Museum of Lancashire (Preston) and Tullie House Museum & Art Gallery Trust (Carlisle). Due to the comparatively large size of Cumbria, and the time it often takes finders to travel through the lakes from the west coast to museums in Carlisle, Penrith or Kendal, the Finds Liaison Officer often meets finders at more local museums at Barrow-in-Furness, Whitehaven or Maryport. The archaeologically significant objects reported to the FLO are all logged on the central PAS database: www.finds.org.uk/database. Access to full records and images can be gained via searching for the find ID: that is the local prefix LANCUM- and the find's own unique six-digit code, e.g. (LANCUM-XXXXXX).

Between 1996 and 2016, 3,570 objects from Cumbria were recorded and promoted to the public database. Approximately one third (1,308) of those are Roman or post-medieval/modern (1,309), and only a few are prehistoric (431) or early medieval in date (64). The recovered archaeological artefacts often come from areas where scheduled archaeological excavation takes places less frequently: hinterland pasture, beaches, former quarries and river valleys. Cumbria is a very rural county and the two national parks – the Lake District National Park and the Yorkshire Dales National Park – take up almost 50 per cent of the county's surface area. The Lake District National Park Authority (LDNPA) have their own archaeological service and, throughout the park, metal-detecting is either strictly prohibited or allowed only with special permission from the LDNPA. This is why most artefacts that are reported from central Cumbria are stone or ceramic artefacts, often found by hikers, walkers or tourists. Metal artefacts from the Lakes are therefore extremely rare and most metal objects are discovered by detectorists searching in the Carlisle area, the Eden Valley, South Lakeland, the Furness peninsula and certain coastal areas in Copeland and Allerdale.

Several of the fifty finds have been acquired by local museums through the 1996 Treasure Act. Treasure includes any metallic object, other than a coin, containing more than 10 per cent precious metal (that is, gold or silver), which is more than 300 years old when found, and any group of two or more prehistoric objects from the same find, regardless of their composition. Also included in the Treasure Act are two or more coins over 300 years old that contain 10 per cent of gold or silver (if the coins contain less than 10 per cent of precious metal, there must be at least ten of them). Any object found in association with Treasure, such as a lead-alloy container or ceramic pot, is considered to be treasure by association. All items of potential Treasure must be reported to the local coroner.

North-west England has traditionally been seen as an area devoid of rural archaeology and beautiful archaeological objects. However, the work of the PAS, alongside recent community, commercial and research excavations, is challenging this assumption. The fifty finds chosen for this book strongly suggest that several areas in Cumbria saw the creation, use and deposition of artefacts that were not only significant for the county, but also for the whole of the north-west region.

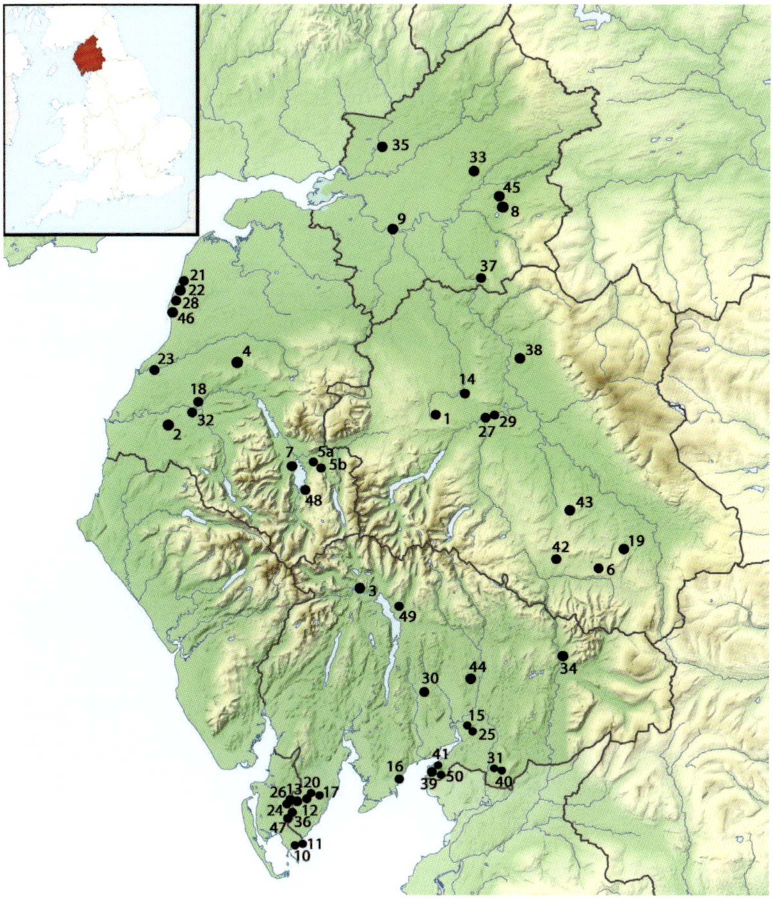

Findspots of the 50 finds from Cumbria.

Chapter 1
Stone Age

There are no Palaeolithic sites in Cumbria, and early hunter-gatherers came to Cumbria about 12,000 years ago. The first evidence for human occupation in Cumbria (lithic blades) was found at Kirkhead Cave in Lower Allithwaite (*c.* 11400–10800 BC), while a human bone and associated lithic material from Kents Bank Cavern suggest a possible early Mesolithic burial. After 10,000 BC, the climate changed; the ice retreated, it became warmer, and Cumbria became heavily wooded. Later Mesolithic (*c.* 8000–4000 BC) material in local museums includes microliths and other lithic objects from the west coast of north Cumbria, including such sites as Drigg, Eskmeals, Williamsons Moss and Monk Moor. The PAS recorded two perforated stone objects, probably hammerstones or maces from Greysouthen (no. 1) and Greystoke (no. 2).

The material from the following Neolithic period (*c.* 4,000–2,500 BC) is mainly characterised by a large number of polished stone axes which originated in the Langdale area of Cumbria. The rock from the Langdales is volcanic tuff, a rock type that is formed from compressed volcanic ash. It has a fine-grained composition and the finished axe heads are predominantly grey/blue-turquoise in colour. Tuff is found in Britain and Ireland in a band that runs down the Irish Sea from the Lake District, County Antrim (Ireland), through North Wales, and into Cornwall and Devon. Volcanic tuff is similar to flint, in that it can be finely worked, ground and polished to form a variety of tools; however, axes are the most common find type, and were used across Northern Europe during the Neolithic period. The finds from Cumbria were mainly reject axes, roughouts (such as nos 3 and 4) and blades created by knapping large lumps of the rock mainly found in the scree slopes of Harrison Stickle and Pike o'Stickle.

Many of the finished axes seem to have been intentionally deposited in moss areas and in rock fissures, a practice that we see repeated in the later Bronze and early Iron Age with bronze axes. The best-known Cumbrian Neolithic site is Ehenside Tarn, near Beckermet (West Cumbria), where both unfinished and polished axes were found, as well as plain bowl pottery, and cattle and deer bones. These finds from Ehenside Tarn (see accompanying figures), and further evidence from the more recently excavated site at Stainton West (Carlisle), strongly suggest that, in Cumbria, we see a continuation of Mesolithic hunter-gatherer activities alongside more settled, agricultural means of living.

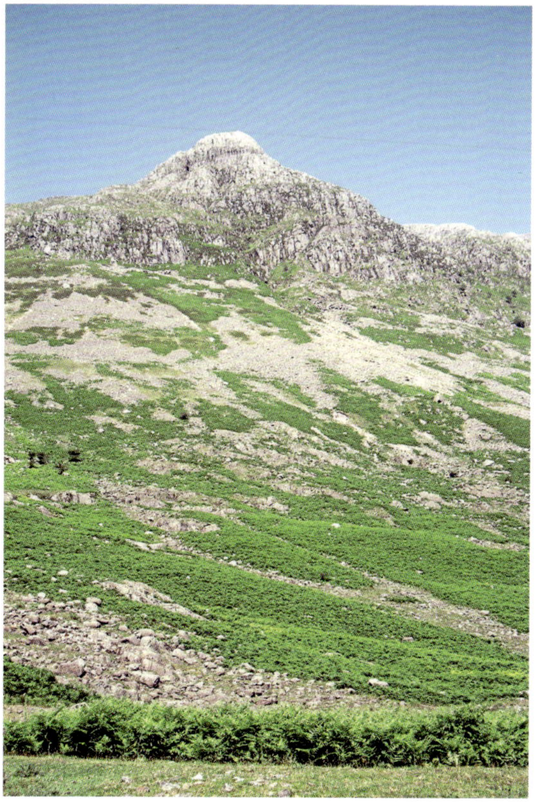

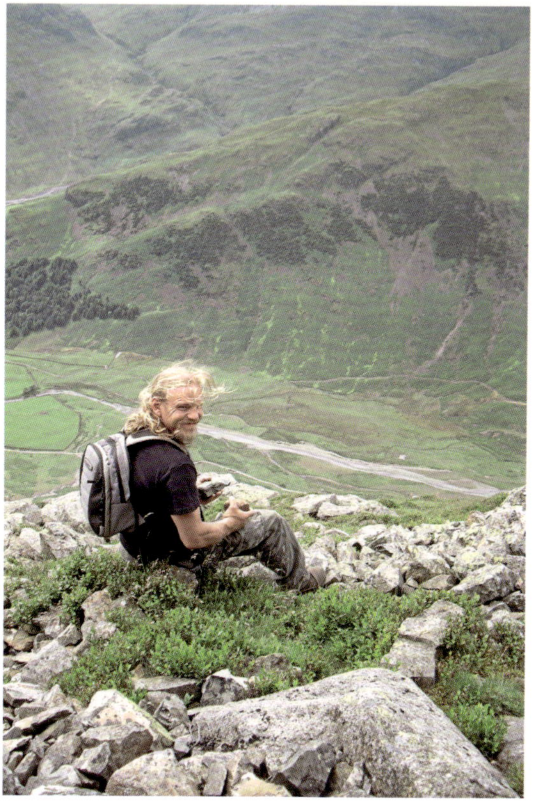

Above left: The peak of Pike O'Stickle in the Langdales. (Jon Adkin)

Above right: Will Lord sitting on the scree slope below Pike o'Stickle looking over Mickleden Valley. (Jon Adkin)

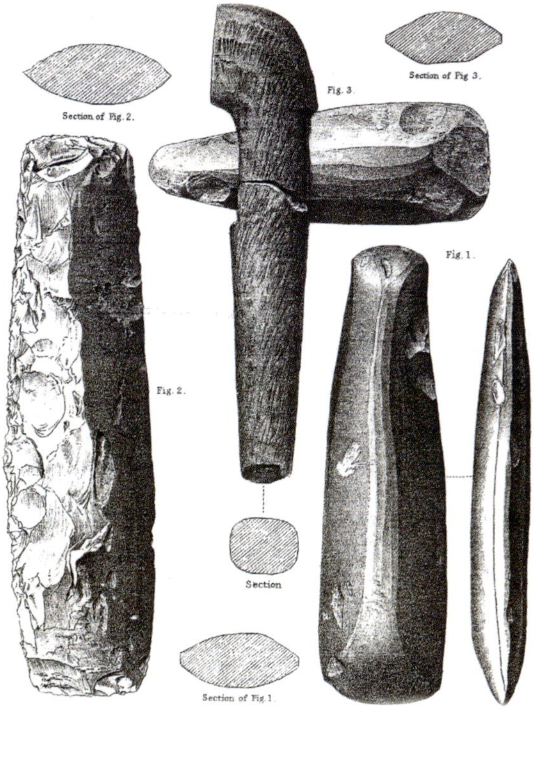

Right: Artefacts recovered from Ehenside Tarn, Cumbria, including a hafted Langdale axe (J. Evans, *Ancient Stone Implements*, London, 1897).

1. Perforated object from the Greystoke area (LANCUM-0FB014)
9000–1000 BC (Early Mesolithic–Late Neolithic)
Length: 82.37 mm; Width: 80.69 mm; Thickness: 32.03 mm; Weight: 308 g

Perforated stone object, probably used as a hammer or mace. It is complete and in good condition, except for a few abrasions around the outer edge. The implement is a simple one, with a generally very uneven doughnut shape and a circular central perforation, which was probably drilled using a bow-like device and a stick with a rounded point, plus water and sand. Dr Kevin Leahy suggests that the material that the axe hammer was made from looks like the quartz dolerite from the Whin Sill, which was used to make axe-hammers during the early Bronze Age. Whin Sill deposits can be found in the North Pennines and Northumberland. Formed of dolerite (a basaltic rock) 295 million years ago, it is part of a sheet of rock stretching from Teesdale along a northerly line to Berwick.

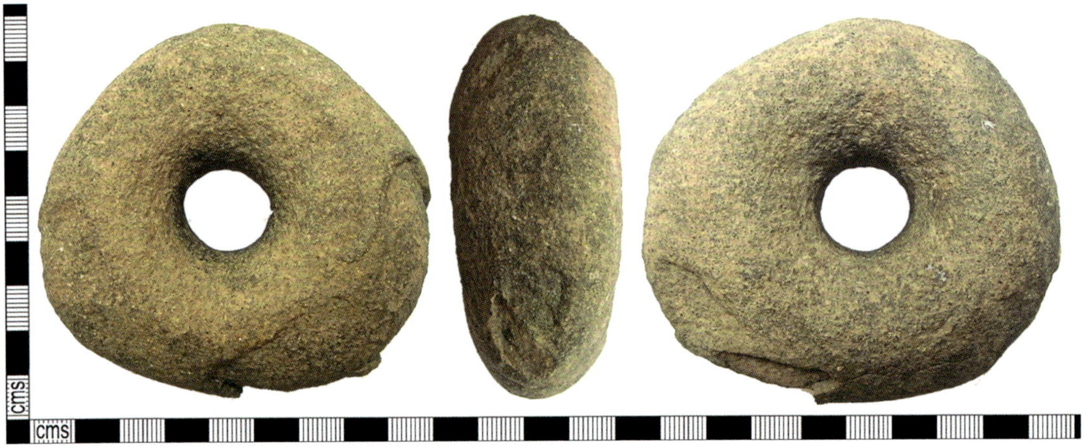

LANCUM-0FB014: Late Mesolithic–Early Neolithic perforated object from the Greystoke area.

2. Perforated unfinished object from the Greysouthen area (LANCUM-35BD37)
9000–2000 BC (Early Mesolithic–Late Neolithic)
Length: 171 mm; Width: 90 mm; Thickness: 95 mm

Large, unfinished perforated object, possibly a hammer or a mace. The object was probably made from a reddish granite, and is roughly triangular in shape, with rounded edges and a very smooth, somewhat polished surface. On the obverse and reverse, the worker had started to perforate the stone but the two holes are not aligned, as can be seen from the side image. Both perforations are only around 2 cm deep and then the work was abandoned, most likely because the holes were not aligned and would not have met in the centre of the mace to create a through hole. The damage/breaks in the stone look recent.

Please note that 1 cm marked on the image is equivalent to 2 cm in real life.

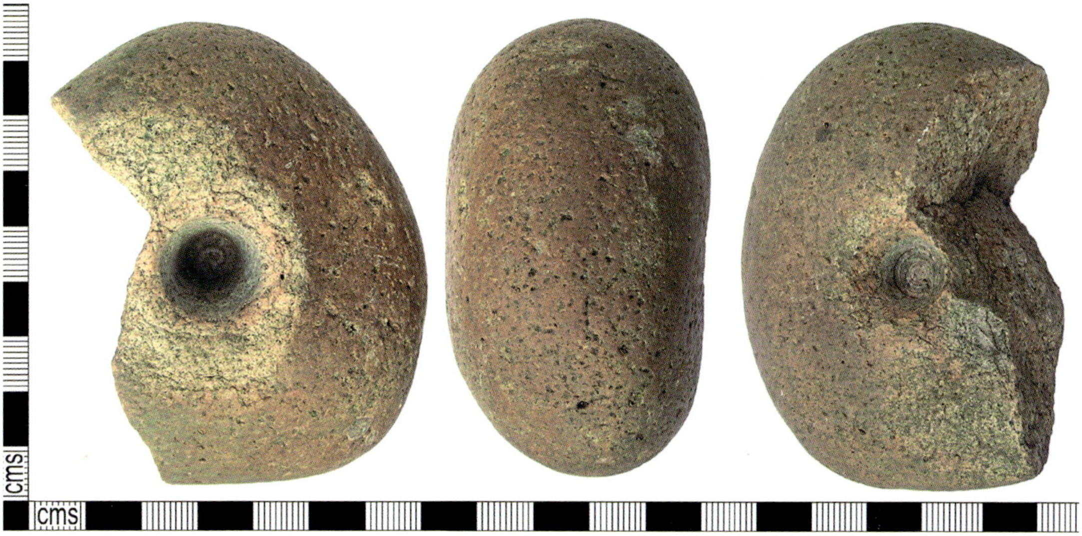

LANCUM-35BD37: Perforated, unfinished object from the Greysouthen area.

3. Langdale roughout from the Ambleside area (LANCUM-4F71B1)
3500–2500 BC (Neolithic)
Length: 182 mm; Width: 67 mm; Thickness: 45 mm

Mid- to late Neolithic axe head roughout, made from a tertiary flake of Langdale tuff. The roughout is thin-butted and double convex in section; it has crudely rounded ends, and expands in plan, from both the butt and the blade end, to reach its maximum width midway along its length. After sourcing the stone, it would have taken a considerable amount of time, (well over thirty-two hours), to finish the axe.

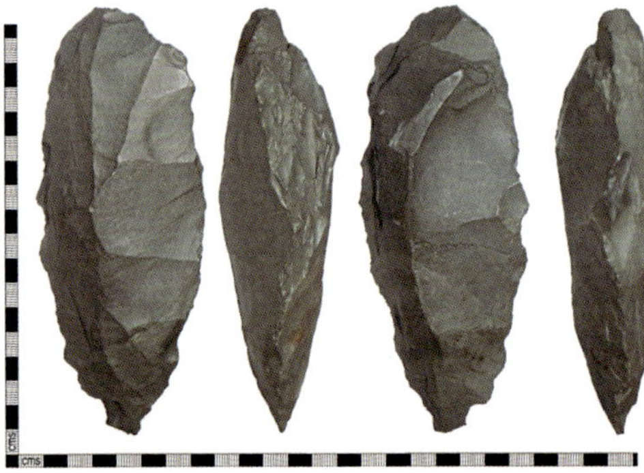

LANCUM-4F71B1: Neolithic Langdale roughout from the Ambleside area.

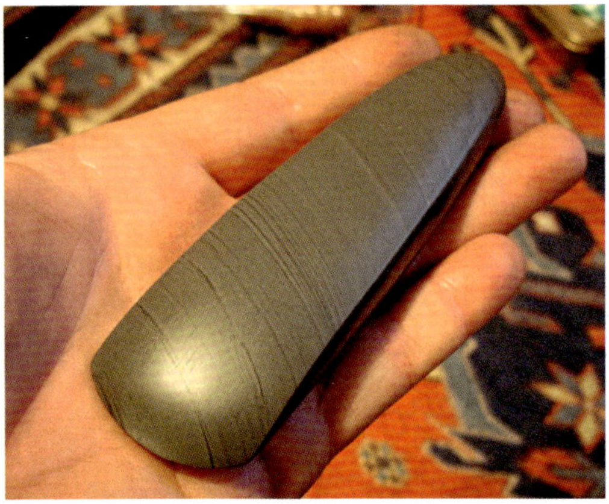

Finished Langdale axe: it took Will Lord thirty-two working hours to produce this polished axe. (Will Lord, Beyond 2000 BC: Prehistoric Experiences)

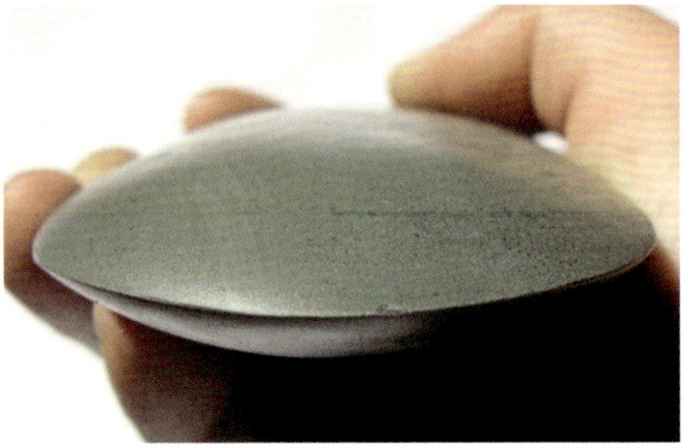

After thirty-two working hours: the blade of a polished Langdale axe, made by Will Lord. (Will Lord, Beyond 2000 BC: Prehistoric Experiences)

4. Langdale roughout from the Sunderland area (LANCUM-A52C63)
3500–2500 BC (Neolithic)
Length: 340 mm; Width: 95 mm

A very large Langdale axe roughout. It survives in very good condition, with only minimal modern damage, which is very fortunate. It had been found by a farmer in one of his fields some time ago and used as a doorstop on the farm ever since. The roughout is thin-butted and double convex in section, and has one crudely rounded and one almost rectangular end. The latter one would have been shaped into the blade. Again, it expands in plan from both the butt and the blade end, with its maximum width occurring about midway along its length.

This roughout, too, would have required many more days' work of shaping and polishing before it was hafted. Discoveries of wooden hafts are extremely rare. However, one haft was found with its axe head still in place at Ehenside Tarn in Cumbria.

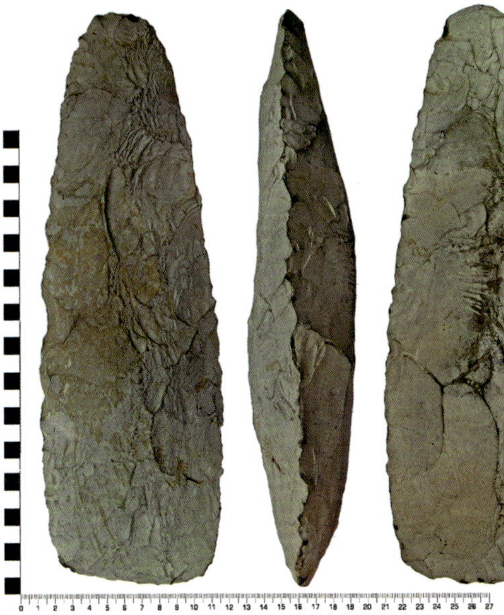

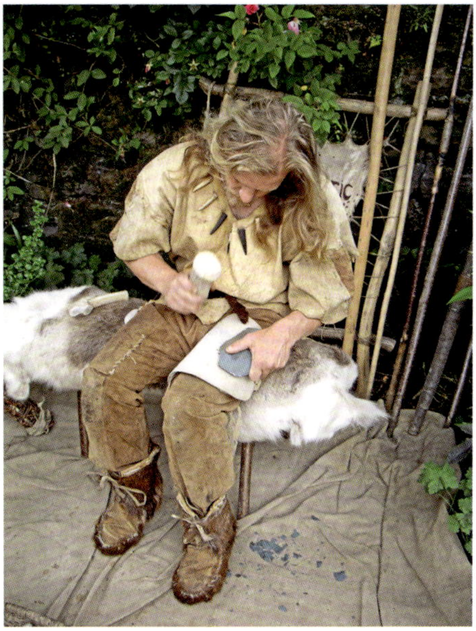

Above left: LANCUM-A52C63: Neolithic Langdale roughout from the Sunderland area.

Above right: Will Lord knapping Sky-blue Langdale tuff. (Copyright Will Lord, Beyond 2000BC: Prehistoric Experiences)

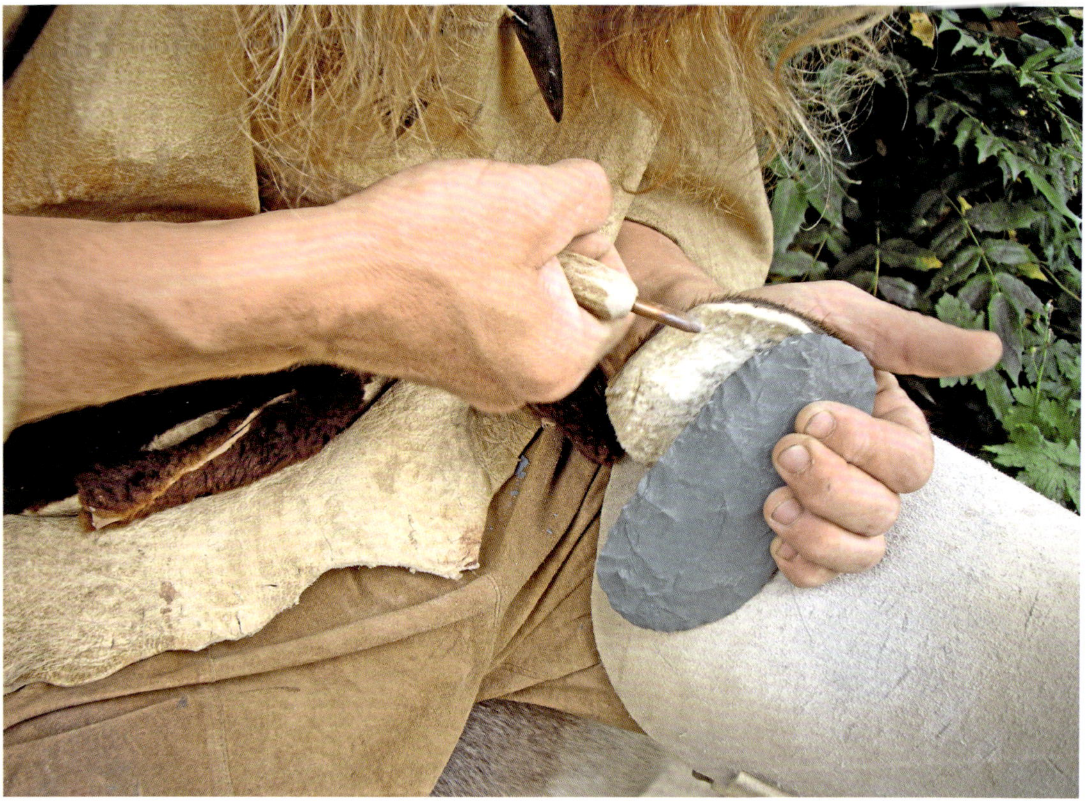

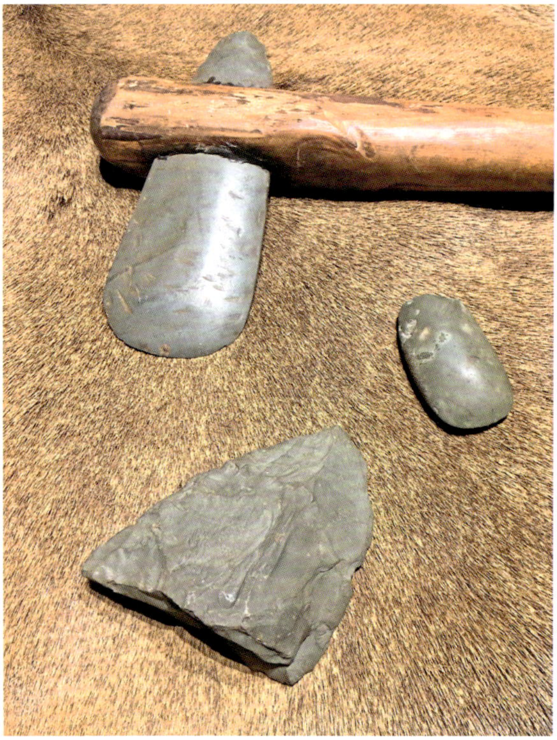

Above: Will Lord working on a Langdale roughout. (Will Lord, Beyond 2000 BC: Prehistoric Experiences)

Left: A piece of Langdale tuff, a small finished axe head and a large hafted axe head. (Replicas made by Will Lord, Beyond 2000 BC: Prehistoric Experiences)

Chapter 2
Bronze Age

By the Bronze Age, settlements in Cumbria had taken a much more permanent form. Like the transition from Mesolithic to Neolithic, the transition from Neolithic to early Bronze Age was gradual, and continuity of sites is likely. A number of Bronze Age flint arrowheads found in Cumbria show the progression of flint-knapping from the Neolithic period (no. 7), while in central Carlisle plough or ard marks have been found at a number of sites beneath Roman levels. Although undated, these features are thought to be of a late Neolithic to early Bronze Age date because of the large lithic assemblages from the same excavations.

Unlike in southern England, where the Neolithic–early Bronze Age transition is marked by the 'Beaker Period', burials with beaker pottery are rare in Cumbria and the north-west. There are only a handful of such burials known from Cumbria, with examples at Clifton, Broomrigg and Hunsonby. The beakers from Ewanrigg and the flat cemetery at Garlands were found in association with collared urns. Other cemeteries that have produced pottery include Aglionby, Maryport, and Aughertree Fell. All of these contain overhanging rim urns. The Bronze Age vessel fragments found in the Keswick area (no. 5) by a farmer digging a land drain are very typical for this type of pottery. If fragmented, they are often not easily recognised as ceramic because they are, although thick-walled, brittle and tempered with large quartzite inclusions. Bronze Age pottery does not normally survive well in Cumbrian soil.

Bronze Age artefacts other than ceramics have been found throughout the county, including: several bronze axe heads from South Lakeland (e.g., from Kendal and Levens); an axe and a sword at Gleaston (Furness); a rapier near the hamlet of Salta (Allerdale); and an intriguing carved granite ball near Carlisle. In the past, most finds of single items of Bronze Age metalwork have come from the Furness peninsula, South Lakeland and the Eden Valley, and this distribution of findspots is mirrored by finds recorded with the PAS. Early Bronze Age metalwork distribution is largely along communication valleys (such as the Eden valley) and on the Furness and West Cumbrian plains, with evidence on the west coast of connections with Ireland, possibly exemplified by the find of a gold lunula fragment (no. 8). Generally, Bronze Age metalwork hoards are rare in Cumbria (notable examples are at Ambleside, Hayton, Fell Lane and Kirkhead Cave) but, after having been reported under the Treasure Act, two further important hoards could be added to the list: Rampside I and II (nos 10 and 11). These date slightly later than the hoard from Ambleside, but show the continued importance of the Furness peninsula as a significant site for prehistoric metalwork deposition in Cumbria.

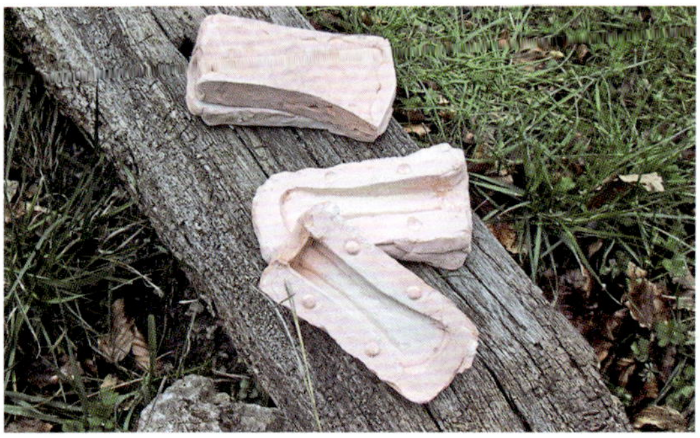

Modern clay moulds for a flanged axe. (Dot Boughton)

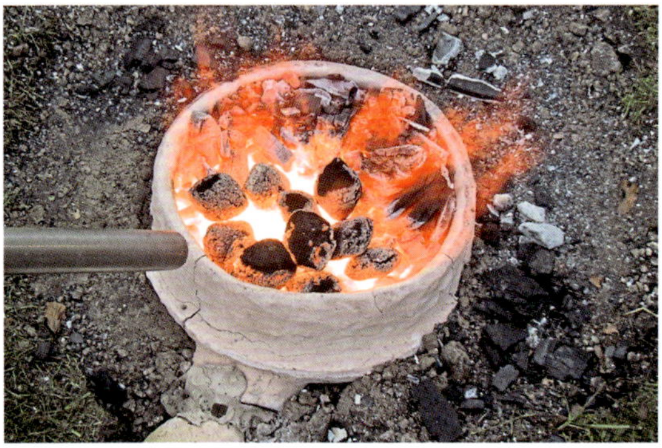

Getting the fire going in the furnace needs a lot of oxygen. (Dot Boughton)

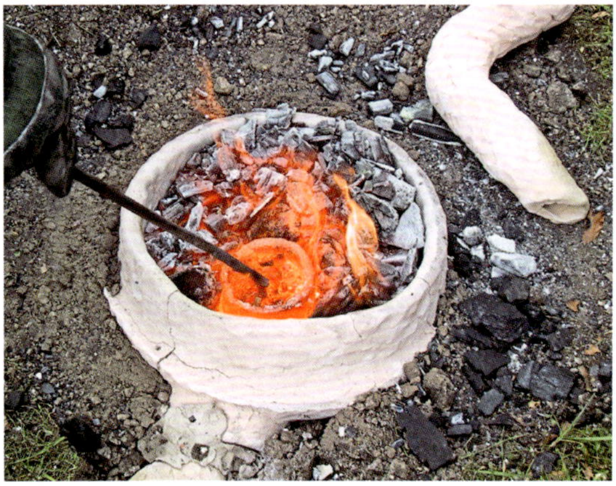

Heating the metal in the crucible. (Dot Boughton)

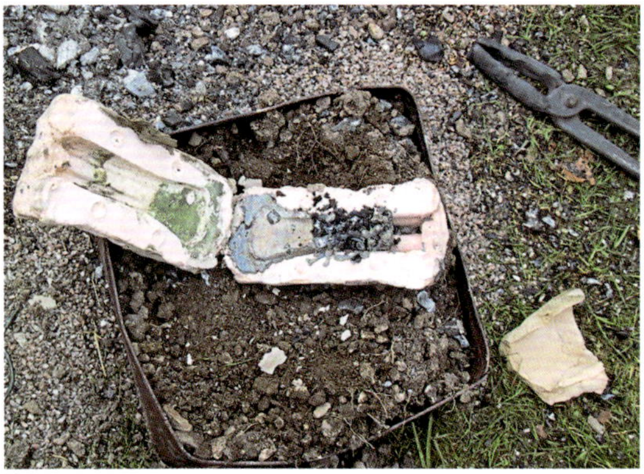

Slightly unsatisfactory result: only half a flanged axe! (Dot Boughton)

5. Bronze Age potsherds from the Keswick area (LANCUM-474FD0 and LANCUM-477B84)
2150–800 BC (Bronze Age)
5a – Length: 100.19 mm; Width: 13.38 mm; Thickness: 16.03 mm; Weight: 130.44 g
5b – Length: 38.72 mm; Width: 36.1 mm; Thickness: 13.67 mm; Weight: 19.95 g

Two sherds of one or, more likely, two handmade earthenware vessels dating from the Bronze Age. The larger sherd comes from the rim of a rim and is comparatively thick and heavy for its size, which is typical for Bronze Age pottery. It was made from very gritty local clay, with many medium-sized and larger inclusions of grit and quartzite. The fabric is rough and the breaks show inclusions of up to 5 mm in diameter.

The second sherd is a small body sherd with equally large inclusions. There is hardly any curvature to it, and what looks like the inside is of an almost black colour, while the outside is light brown. The inside is plain, but the outside is decorated with at least three very crude horizontal lines. The upper and lower lines coincide with the breaks. The curvature of the sherd is unusual, in so far that what looks like the inside (the 'the black side') is convex rather than concave, while the outside is convex. However, the sherd may have come from the part of the vessel that lies between the shoulder and the rim. Considering the probable diameter of the sherd, it probably came from a wide-rimmed vessel and it is probable that the vessel was very heavy when complete.

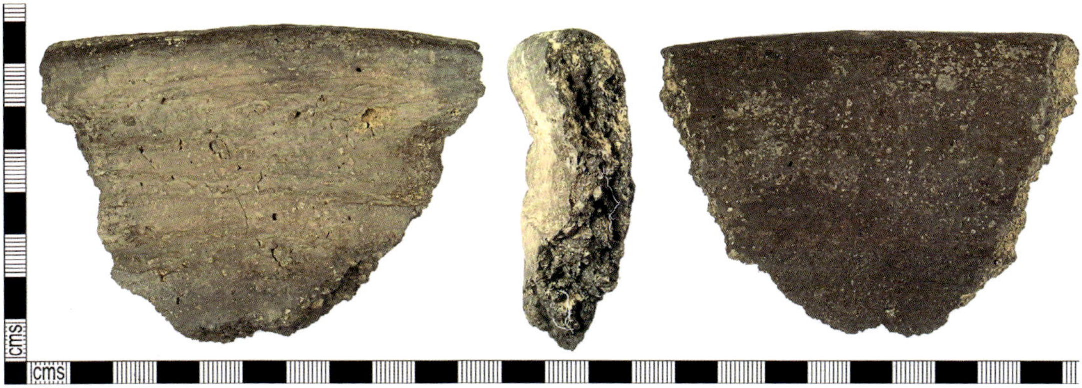

LANCUM-474FD0: Bronze Age potsherd from the Keswick area.

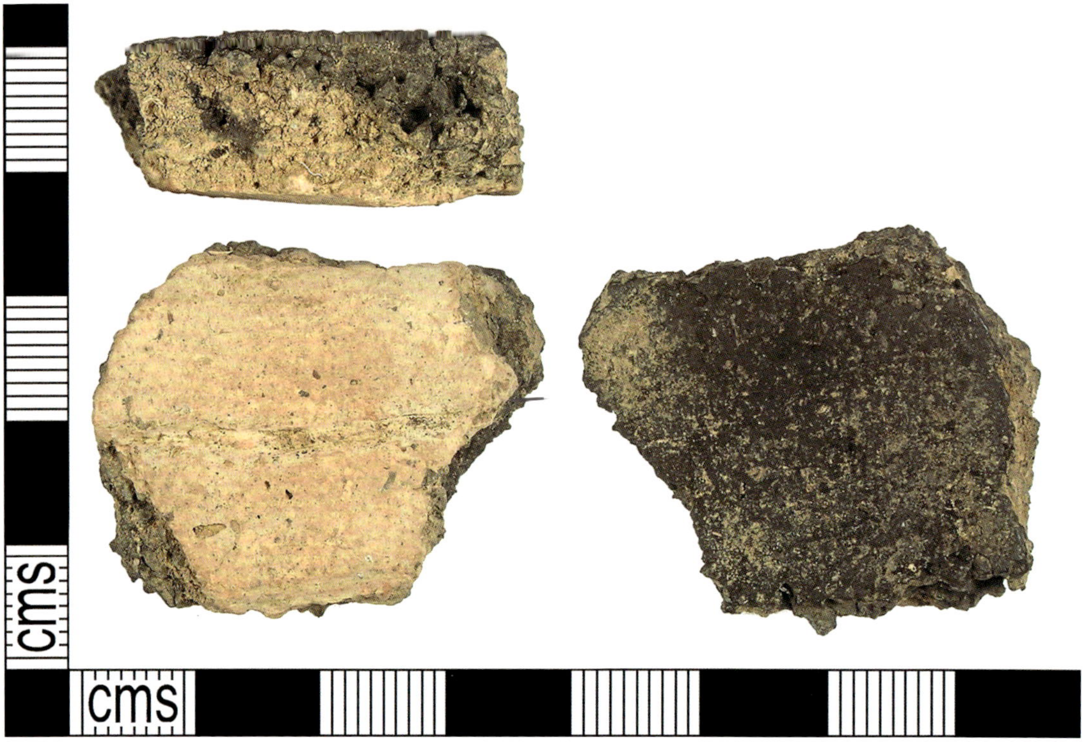

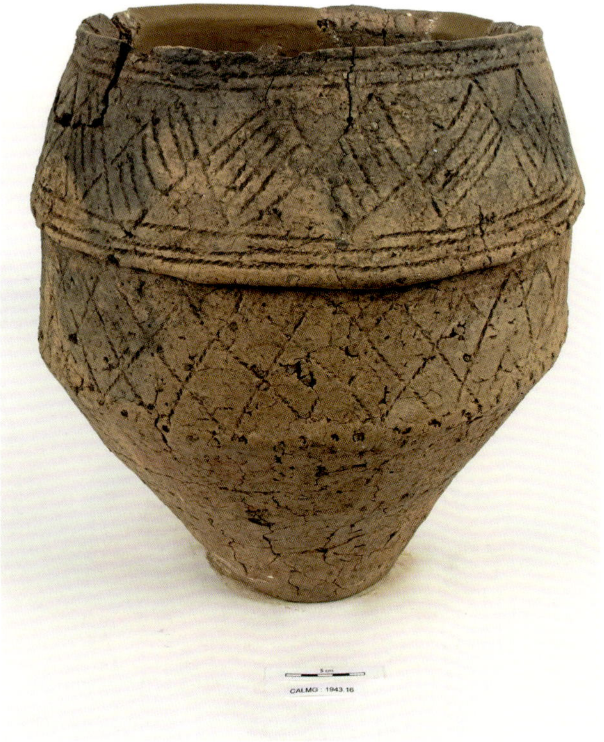

Above: LANCUM-477B84: Bronze Age potsherd from the Keswick area.

Left: The Bronze Age urn from Holmrook Hall. (Tullie House Museum & Art Gallery Trust)

6. Jet bead from Crosby Garrett (LANCUM-AF6483)
2500–1500 BC (Early Bronze Age)
Length: 58 mm; Width: 30.4 mm; Thickness: 6.5 mm; Weight: 29.7 g

One half of a large spacer bead made from black jet or shale. The bead is very large and shows secondary working. Both primary and secondary worked edges are worn smooth. It is convex in profile, which suggests that it started off as a large oval bead with a circular cross-section and a single perforation along its long axis. It is possible that it broke in two when the long perforation was drilled. After splitting into two or more pieces, two more holes were drilled, each one towards one the bead's short edges. These holes are also very worn, and may indicate that the bead was worn on a necklace, possibly as the centrepiece, as suggested by the shape and direction of wear.

Jet is a type of lignite, a precursor to coal, and is considered to be a minor gemstone. It is not a mineral as such, but has an organic origin, being derived from decaying wood under extreme pressure. Jet is best known as the material from which the Early Bronze Age spacer bead jet necklaces were made. This bead resembles larger spacer beads in size and material, but not in shape. There is only one other jet bead recorded from Cumbria: a complete bead from the Eden area (LANCUM-46FBD2).

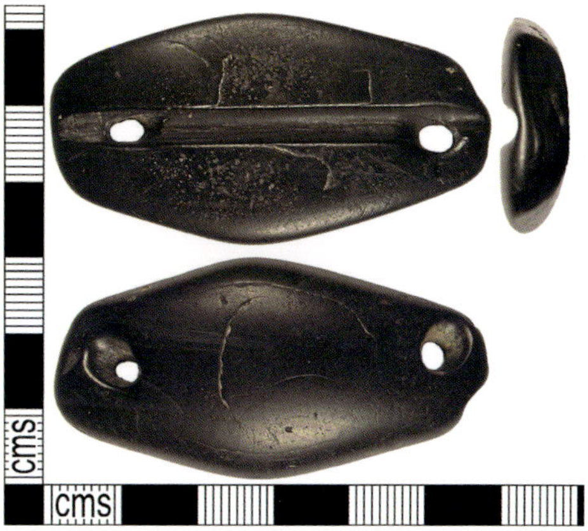

Right: LANCUM-AF6483: Early Bronze Age jet bead from Crosby Garrett.

Below: LANCUM-46FBD2: a complete jet bead from the Eden area.

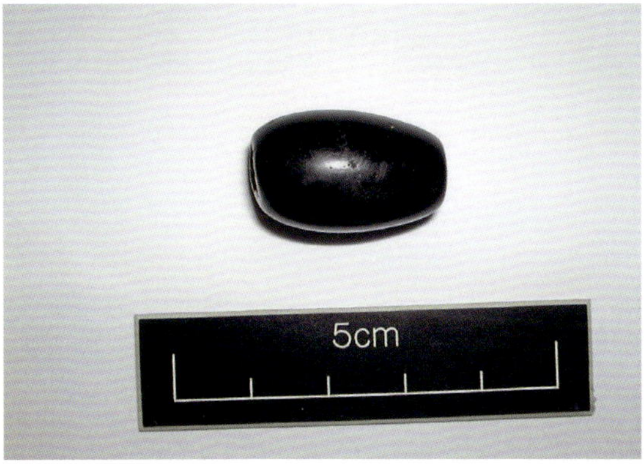

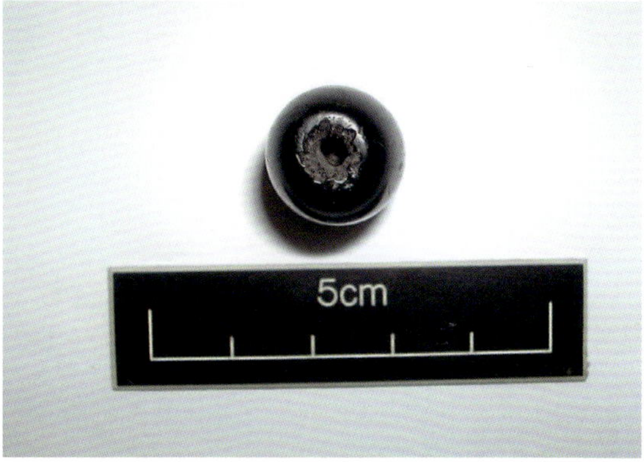

7. Bronze Age arrowhead from Derwent Water (LANCUM-DECB54)

2150–1500 BC (Early Bronze Age)
Length: 29.51 mm; Width: 24.46 mm; Thickness: 4.17 mm; Weight: 2.5 g

Barbed and tanged flint arrowhead, dating from the Early Bronze Age. It is broadly sub-triangular in plan and lentoid in cross-section. The arrowhead has been knapped from a honey-coloured piece of flint. It was manufactured using a number of different techniques, including direct and indirect percussion, as well as pressure/ripple flaking, which can be seen on both surfaces. It is symmetrical in shape and undamaged. Both sides of the arrowhead have been retouched to create sharp edges. However, one barb has a square, unfinished-looking terminal, while the other has a finely knapped and retouched rounded end, which is clearly finished. It is likely that the arrowhead was unfinished when it was lost or deposited in the lake, but it could have also been used in its unfinished state if needed, and could thus have been a hunting loss. Its fresh, crisp condition, without patination or weathering, suggests burial until recent exposure.

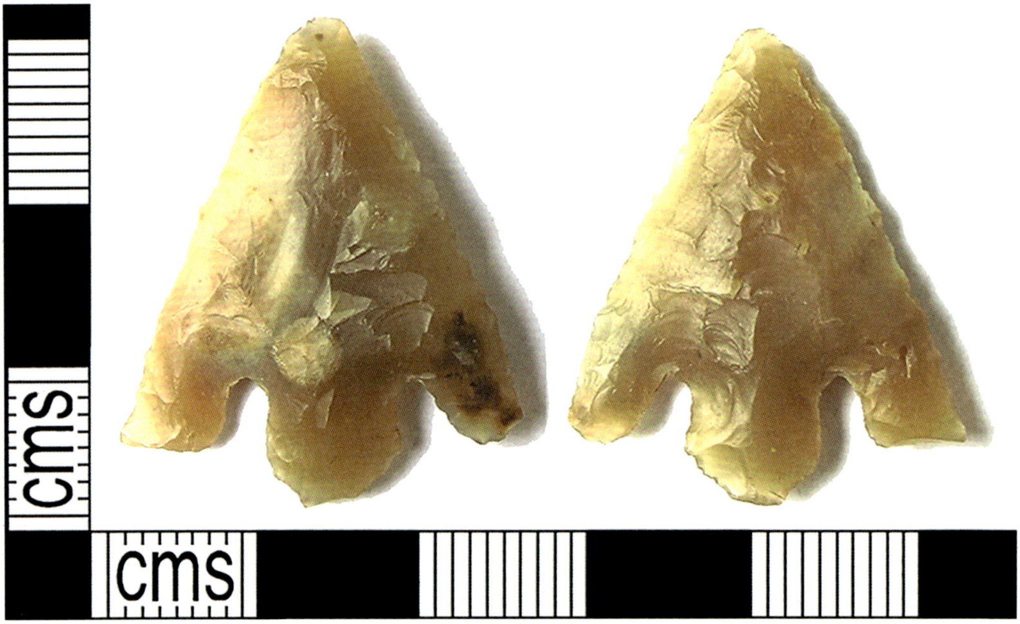

LANCUM-DECB54: Early Bronze Age flint arrowhead from Derwent Water.

8. Lunula terminal from the Brampton area (LANCUM-449151)
2200–2100 BC (Early Bronze Age)
Length: 47.48 mm; Width: 25.97 mm; Thickness: 0.63 mm; Weight: 6.88 g

The lunula terminal is complete yet somewhat bent, the only break showing where it broke off from the main part of the broad, crescent-shaped collar. The terminal (or 'horn') consists of a flat part shaped like the bowl of a spoon, which is connected by a short 'stalk' to an elongated part with a flat-rectangular cross-section; this would have extended into the large, crescent-shaped collar. The bowl-shaped end is undecorated on both sides, but the strip displays a decoration of parallel lines on the obverse, while being undecorated on the reverse. The 'stalk' has a round cross-section and is twisted at a 90-degree angle (as the other terminal or 'horn' would have been). This was necessary for the two terminals to interlock when the lunula was worn.

Although common in Ireland, lunulae are very rare early Bronze Age gold objects found in the British Isles and north-west France. Only few are known from Scotland, and this is the first lunula fragment from Cumbria. A small number have also been found in Cornwall and Brittany, France. In contrast to some of the Scottish lunulae and our fragment from Brampton, original Irish lunulae were made from extremely thin gold sheet (less than 0.1-mm thick). They are very fragile and much less substantial than these thicker lunulae, which are classified as 'provincial-type lunulae'. Original Irish sheet lunulae were so thin that they could be rolled and folded, but the fragment from Brampton was made from a thicker sheet of gold. 'Provincial' lunulae, like the example from Brampton, are usually decorated with an untidy pattern of parallel lines and 'boxes', and dotted with elongated, square and round punches making up lines, zigzag lines or bundles of short, incised lines. All decoration is geometrical and not figural.

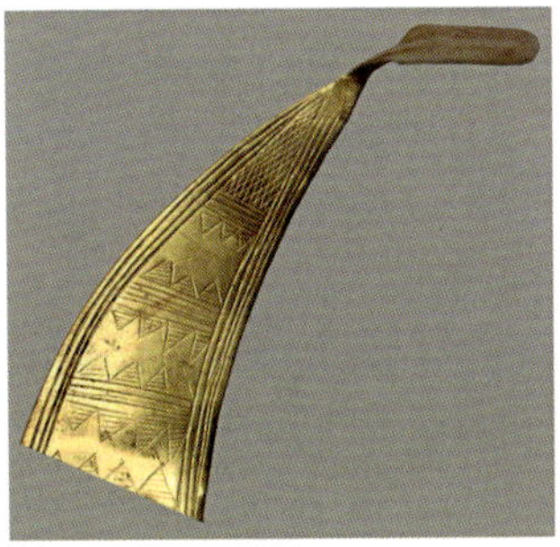

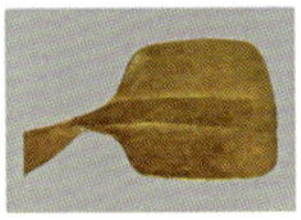

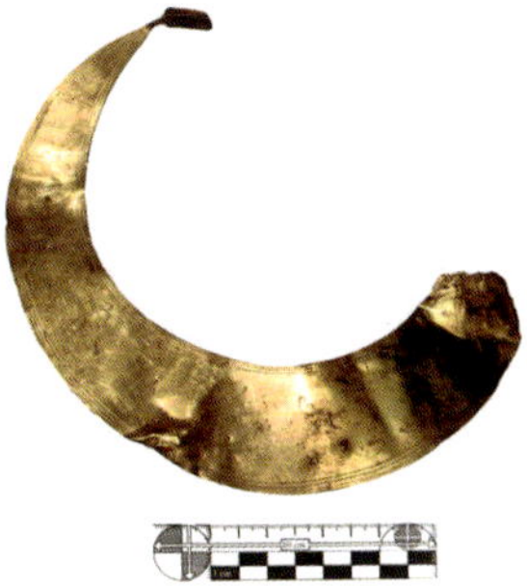

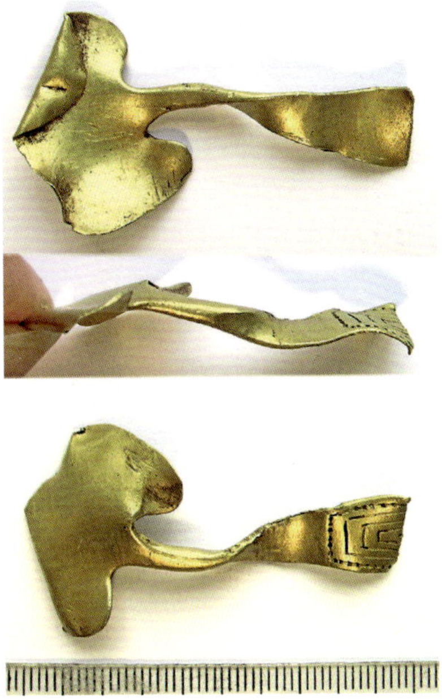

Above: A complete lunula found in the Tarrant Valley, Dorset, recorded as DOR-2198F8.

Right: LANCUM-449151: Gold lunula terminal from the Brampton area.

9 Flanged axe from the Carlisle area (LANCUM-0D2405)
1500–1300 BC (Middle Bronze Age)
Length: 143.27 mm; Width: 58.26 mm; Thickness: 35.17 mm; Weight: 431 g

The axe is of the flanged type; with its small stop-ridge, it could possibly be related to the shield-pattern palstaves of the Acton Park metalwork assemblage, to which it bears a clear resemblance. The axe is a heavy implement, complete with the two flanges and a still-sharp, crescent-shaped blade. It has a dull brown/gold patina and is, overall, in very good shape. The surface on the lower part of the blade looks quite worn, however, and, due to some patches of black patina, it is difficult to tell if there are any signs of wear (e.g., indentations or re-sharpening marks) on the surface. The axe was probably cast in a two-piece clay mould.

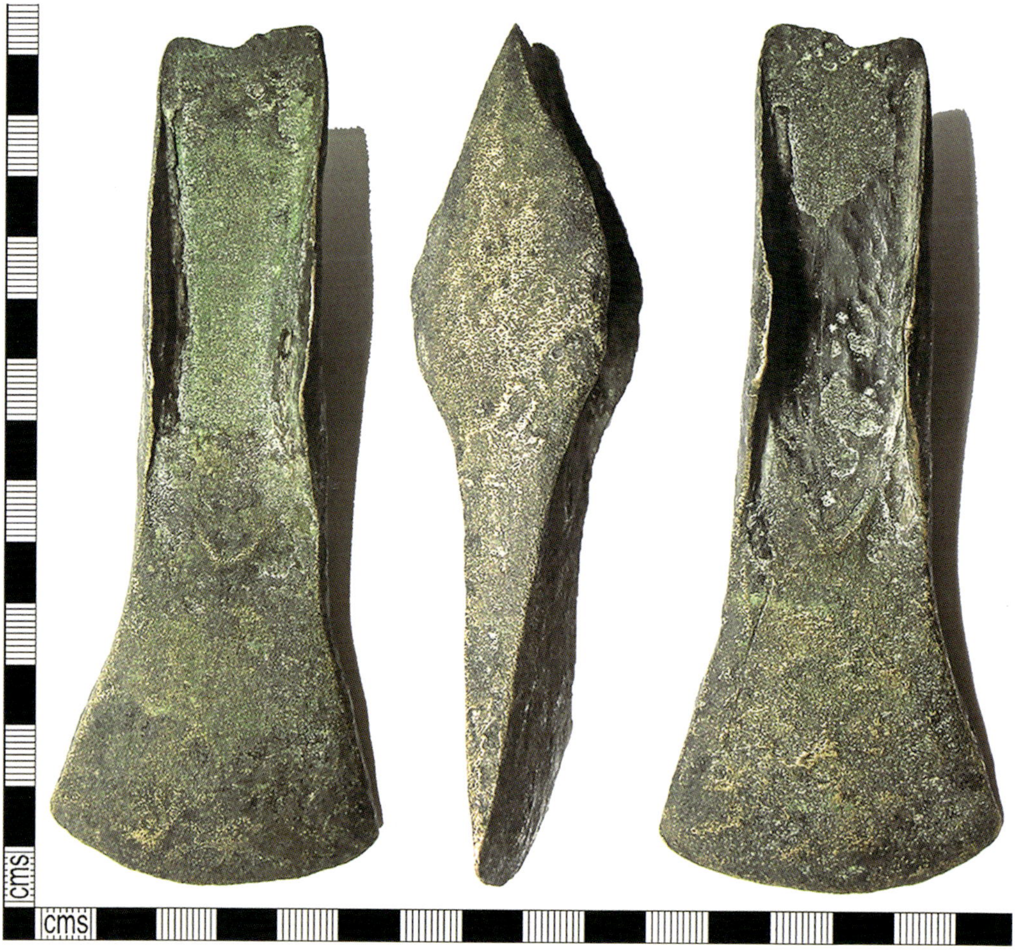

LANCUM-0D2405: Middle Bronze Age flanged axe from the Carlisle area.

10. Late Bronze Age Hoard from Rampside I (LANCUM-428850)
1150–900 BC (Late Bronze Age)

Late Bronze Age hoard, comprising two socketed axes; one, or possibly two, socketed gouges; seven sword fragments of one, or possibly two, weapons; two fragments of what was probably a flesh-hook terminal; and two small pieces of casting jet.

The first socketed axe appears to be of Type Fulford, which dates from the middle part of the late Bronze Age (Wallington/Wilburton metalwork assemblages) and typically shows Irish influence in its multiple collar mouldings. They are normally found in northern Britain, and the closest parallel to the piece from Rampside was found at Low Fell in the Langdales, Cumbria. The second socketed axe is probably of Type Dowris and had a second object, probably a socketed gouge, inserted into its socket. Socketed, collared gouges like this one – and the complete one, which was also part of the hoard – are very common in late Bronze Age hoards of both the Wallington/Wilburton and Ewart Park metalwork traditions.

Hoards such as the one from the Rampside area, comprising fragments of sword, socketed gouges, socketed axes and casting jets/waste, are relatively common features of the late Bronze Age in southern England. The insertion of objects into the sockets of axes is also a common practice in hoards of this period. Hoards of this size are, however, still relatively rare in northern England, and there are no comparable finds from Lancashire or Cumbria currently known.

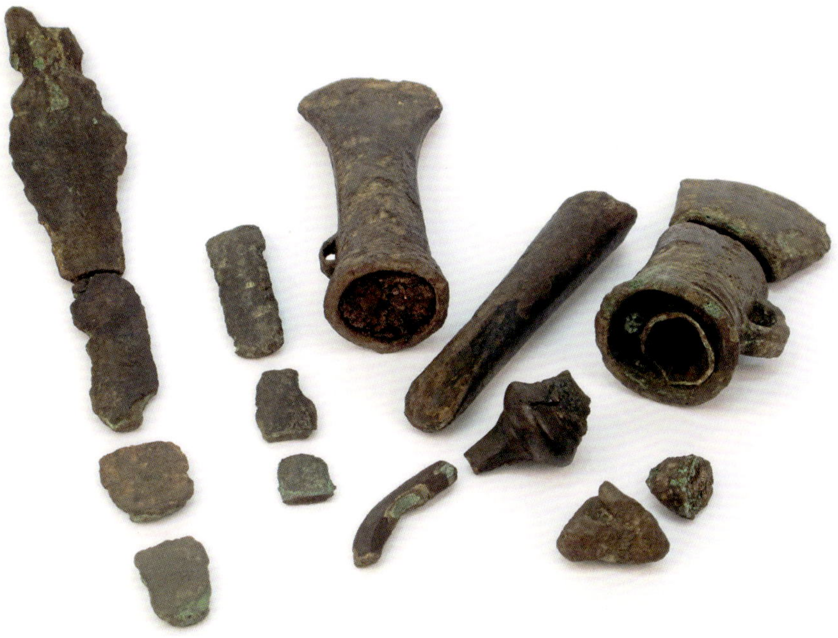

LANCUM-428850: Late Bronze Age hoard from Rampside I.

11. Late Bronze Age Hoard from Rampside II/Roosecote (LANCUM-4118A0)

1150–900 BC (Late Bronze Age)

A hoard of eight artefacts: two socketed axes, one large spearhead (in two fragments), two small flat chisels (which were discovered in socketed axe 2), a rapier-blade fragment inside a hollow-head spearhead (which was discovered in socketed axe 1) and a chape fragment (in two pieces).

This second late Bronze Age hoard from Rampside is a small assemblage of eight artefacts. The large spearhead is broken in two: the edges along the break are rough and the body of the spearhead is slightly bent. It looks as if it was purposefully bent and the tip broken off before deposition. The scabbard chape survives only incomplete; it was also broken in two pieces, but the edge wear suggests that the breaks were old. The hoard also included two socketed axes: one undecorated, socketed looped axe, probably of Type Dowris, and a decorated, socketed looped axe of Type Ulleskelf, which are rare – only four examples are known from the north of England. The other axe is of a baggier shape, which suggests an Irish influence.

Both axes' sockets were used as receptacles for smaller items of metalwork: two small woodworking tools, possibly chisels, were inside the Ulleskelf Type axe and a probable rapier/dirk-blade fragment had been stuffed inside the Dowris Type axe. The rapier/dirk-blade fragment could not be further identified because it is firmly jammed inside a small fragment of a hollow-blade spearhead. The spearhead fragment was jammed into the socket of the axe diagonally, as scratch marks on the inside of the axe socket show (see finder's images). Small items of metalwork are often found inside sockets of socketed axes. This was either for the possible safekeeping of smaller items of bronze, perhaps for recycling, or else, if it was a votive deposition, to render the axe useless, because it would now no longer be possible to haft it. The latter seems more likely in this case, as the spearhead from Rampside II shows signs of ritual destruction: it was bent until the tip snapped off, which is suggested by the break and the slight curve in the upper part of the head.

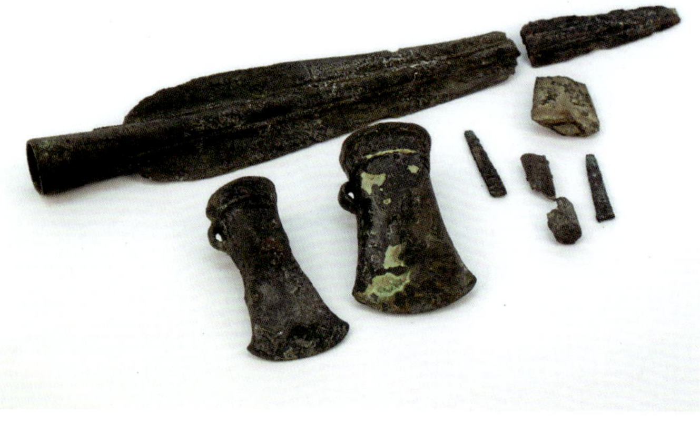

LANCUM-4118A0: Late Bronze Age hoard from Rampside II/Roosecote.

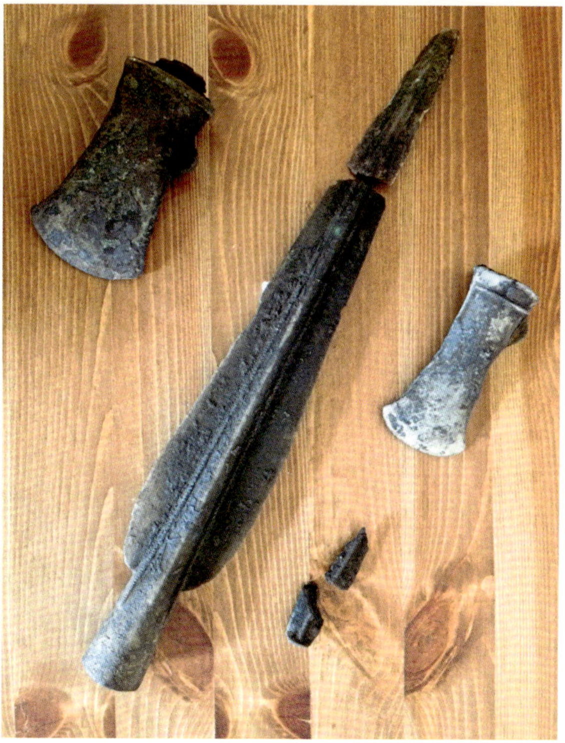

Right: LANCUM-4118A0: Late Bronze Age hoard from Rampside II/Roosecote (Finder's Image).

Below: Dowris Type axe from Rampside II, with spearhead and rapier fragment inside socket (Finder's Image).

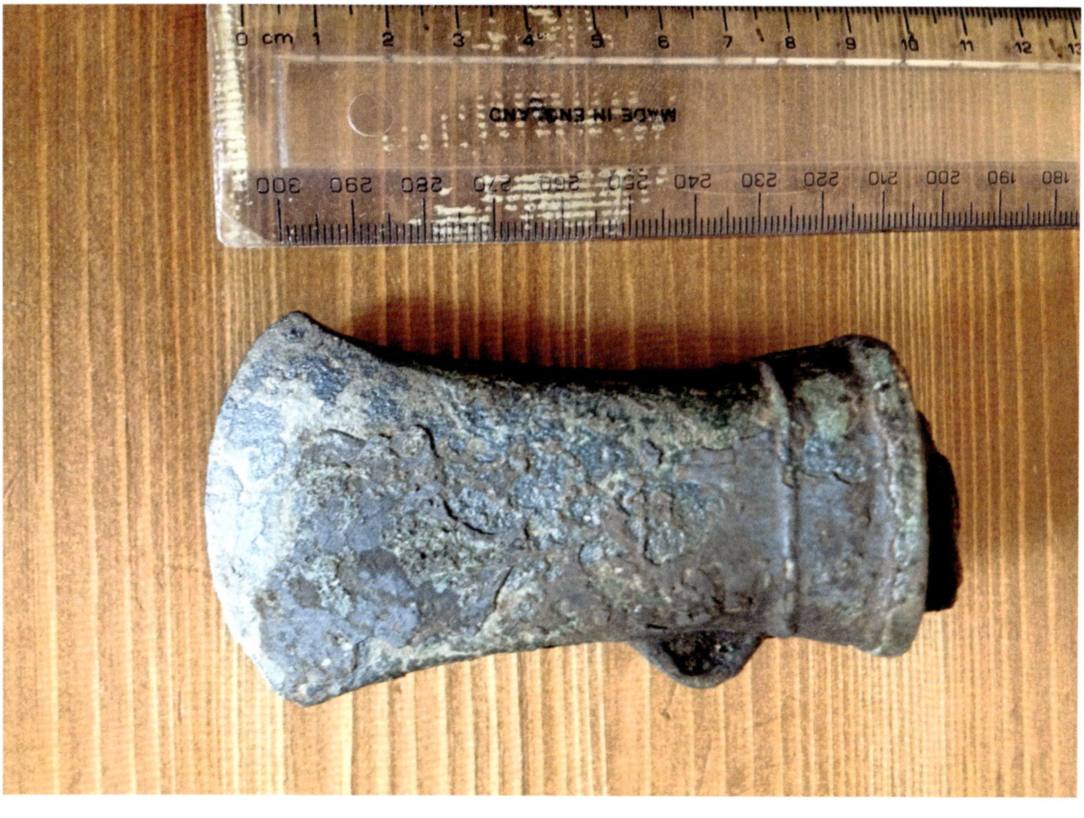

Chapter 3
Iron Age

One of the greatest problems for Iron Age archaeology in Cumbria is the scarcity of evidence, and an alleged poverty of material culture. Pottery is a rarity on most excavated sites and is, indeed, absent from many. No Iron Age pottery or stone artefacts have been recorded with the PAS so far. Metal finds that can be securely dated to the period are rare, too, although recent research into finds recorded with the PAS and reported under the Treasure Act confirms that small-scale metalwork deposition continued well into the early Iron Age in the Furness peninsula (nos 12 and 13). However, while the two late Bronze Age hoards from Rampside were found on the coast, the deposition of the two early Iron Age hoards is further inland, near the site of Skelmore Heads, perhaps suggesting a prolonged use of the monument. Generally, discoveries of Iron Age metalwork in Cumbria are confined to the southern part of the region – that is, the Furness peninsula and South Lakeland. These scattered finds may possibly suggest an Iron Age society living in relatively small, dispersed settlements. Pollen analysis confirms that the once inhospitable landscape, dominated by dense forests, saw extensive episodes of clearance. This probably resulted in the development of local agricultural and industrial economies, which were, in the Iron Age, more vibrant than was once thought. This suggests that at least some tribal societies were, on the eve of the Roman invasion, more hierarchical and, indeed, organised in their activities. However, unlike southern and eastern English tribes, Iron Age communities in Cumbria did not mint their own coins and the gold stater from Heversham (no. 15) is only one of two recorded from Cumbria.

Classical authors, who are notoriously vague over matters of chronology and location of certain native tribes, and who are, in any case, given to stereotyping in their treatment of barbarians, have left us a collection of tribal names, but little else to facilitate the unravelling of the political, social and economic structures of the Britons who inhabited Cumbria before the Roman period. In the later Iron Age, the principal tribe occupying territory in northern England was called the Brigantes, a name that probably refers to either their upland location or their overlordship. The Roman historian Tacitus, who wrote in the late first century AD, described this northern British tribe as the most populous in Britain. Meanwhile, according to Ptolemy, who derived his information from later first- and second-century military sources, their territory stretched from 'sea to sea', thus probably covering most of the area between the Solway and the Humber. In the later Roman period, the tribe occupying northern Cumbria are known as the Carvetii (possibly a semi-independent subgroup of the Brigantes) with, possibly, another tribe called the Setanii living in South Cumbria.

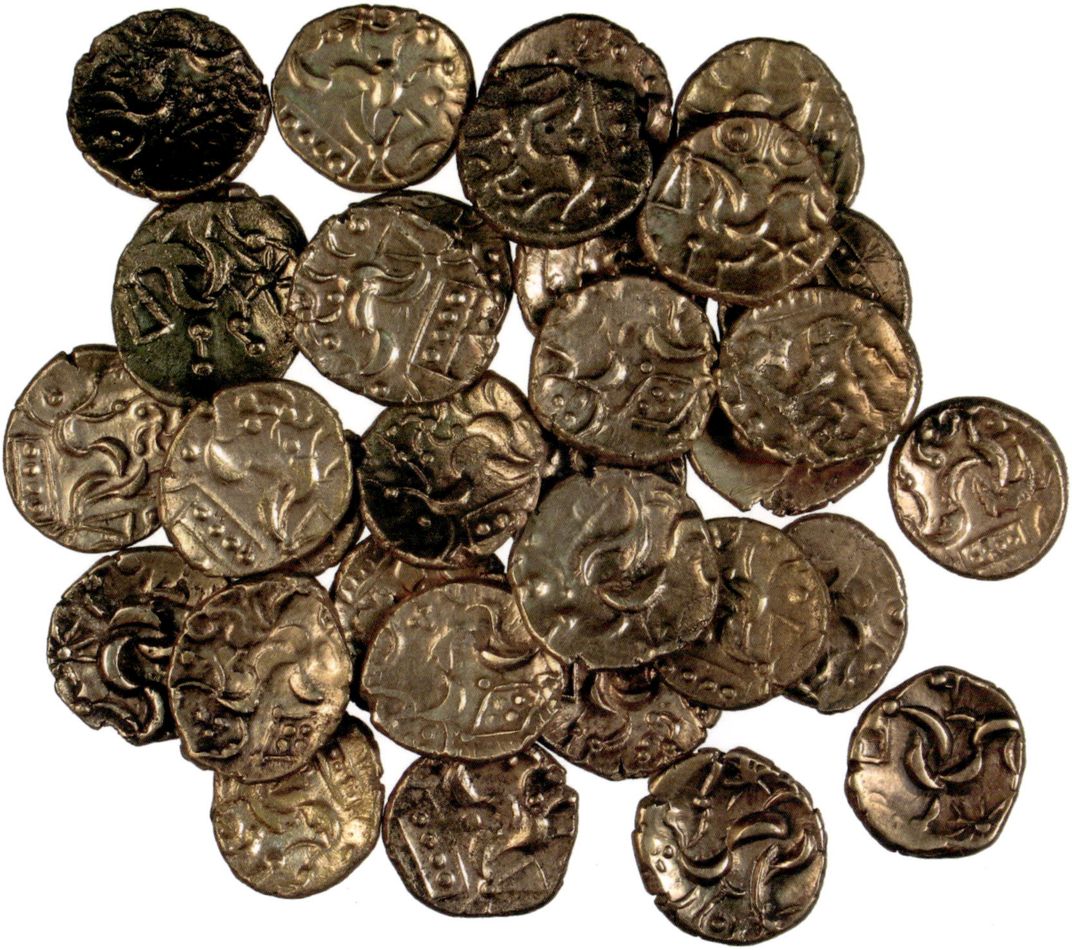

The Lichfield (Staffordshire) hoard of Iron Age coins of the 'North Eastern' regional series, which is often ascribed to the Corieltavi tribe.

12. Socketed axes from the Skelmore Heads area (LANCUM-A9ECA6 and HAMP-5723E3)
800–600 BC (Early Iron Age)
12a – Length: 113 mm; Width of blade: 65 mm; Weight: 305 g
12b – Length: 114.4 mm; Width of blade: 55.7 mm; Weight: 242 g

Two complete cast copper-alloy socketed axes of the Sompting Type, Tower Hill variant. Both axe heads have a shiny smooth patina and are dark brown in colour. They are both undecorated and in very good condition. They have prominent mouth mouldings and the casting seams have been removed. The side loops are oblong in shape and somewhat spurred at the bottom. There are a few smaller nicks and one longer dent in the cutting edge; but these may not have been accidental but intentional damage.

The two axes are not recent discoveries, and have been in their owners' family for over a century. The family originates from Cumbria but, while one brother moved to Hampshire, the other now lives in Lincolnshire. The brothers thought that the axes came from Ulpha in Cumbria, but photographic evidence proves that the axes, along with four others, were discovered near Skelmore Heads in South West Cumbria in 1902. The six socketed axes were all found lying together in a limestone fissure but, after their discovery, four axes were lost and only two remain in museum collections today: Dock Museum, Barrow-in-Furness (Acc. No. 07909) and the Swanson-Cowper collection at Lancaster City Museum (Lancaster, currently on loan to the Ruskin Museum, Coniston, Cumbria).

In the original account of their discovery, it was reported that a workman had found the axes while quarrying limestone in a field near Urswick, Furness. The axes were lying

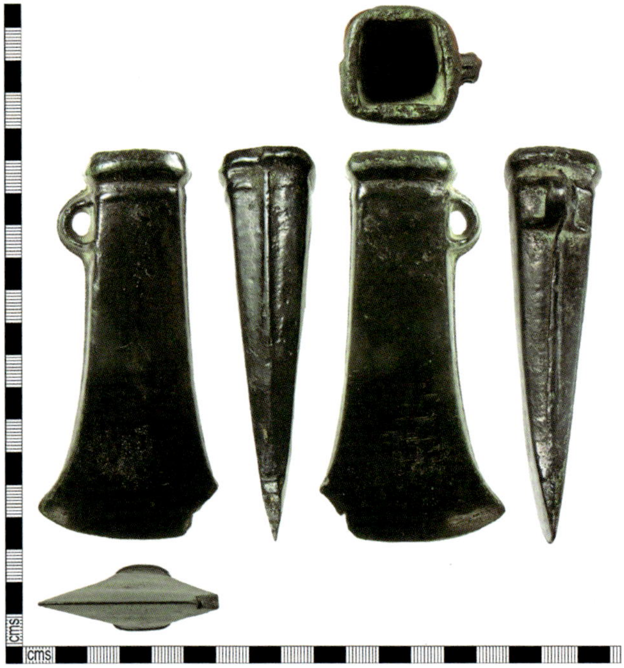

HAMP-5723E3: Early Iron Age socketed axe from the Skelmore Heads hoard.

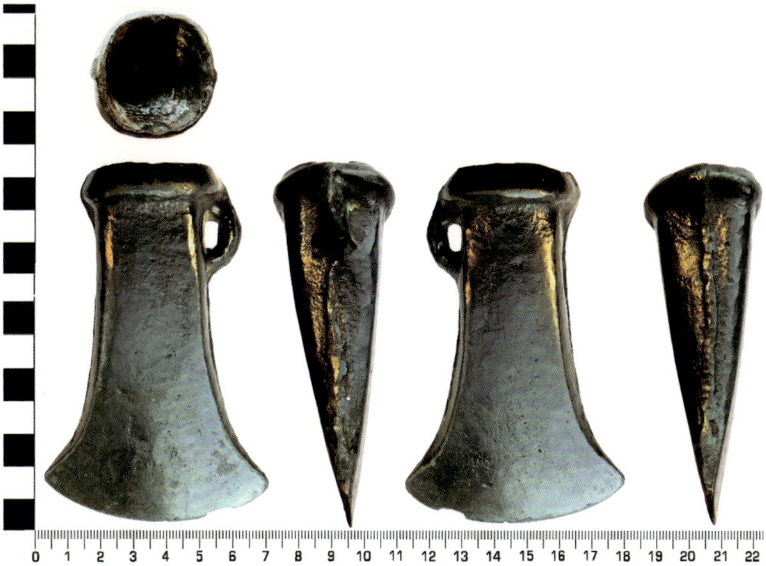

LANCUM-A9ECA6: Early Iron Age socketed axe from the Skelmore Heads hoard.

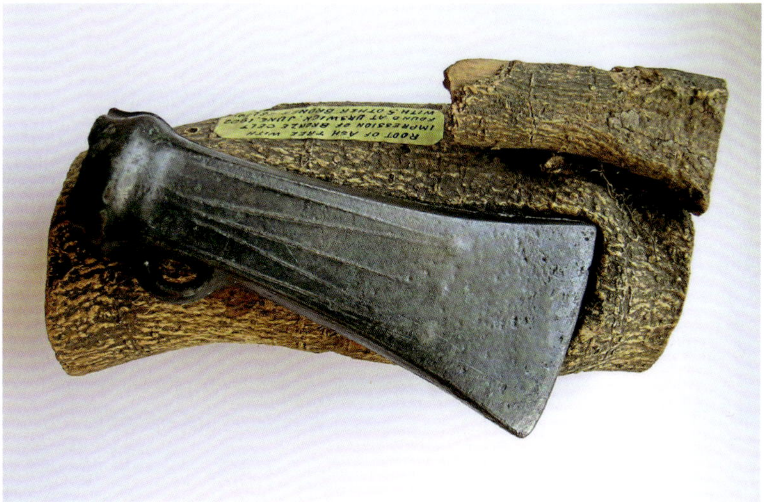

Early Iron Age socketed axe and tree root from the Skelmore Heads hoard (Dock Museum, Barrow-in-Furness, Acc. No: 07909).

together in a fissure between two large blocks of limestone, with the root of an ash tree growing in the fissure bearing an impression of one of the axe heads (both the axe and the root are now in the Dock Museum). The account further says that, while two axes were plain, the other four bore ornaments made up of ribs, pellets and rings. One of the ornamented specimens was not quite perfect; one of the others has been cracked across one face and has a hole near the loop, evidently a defect in casting; another was left in as-cast condition, its cutting edge being half a centimetre thick. In 1902, five of the axes were photographed, while the sixth had been taken to the local pub, the General Burgoyne Inn, and exchanged for a bottle of liquor by the finder. This is the axe that is now in the Ruskin Museum (Coniston), on loan from Lancaster City Museum.

13. Early Iron Age hoard from the Ulverston area (LANCUM-335E04)
800–600 BC (Early Iron Age)

The small hoard from Ulverston consists of three socketed bronze axes of Sompting Type, which were found not far from the findspot of the Skelmore Heads hoard (see above, no. 12). While the smallest and most worn axe is undecorated, the other two are decorated on each face with a central rib, terminating in a pellet-in-circlet with a hanging triangle to the left and right. The points of the triangles are also terminating in a pellet-in-circlet.

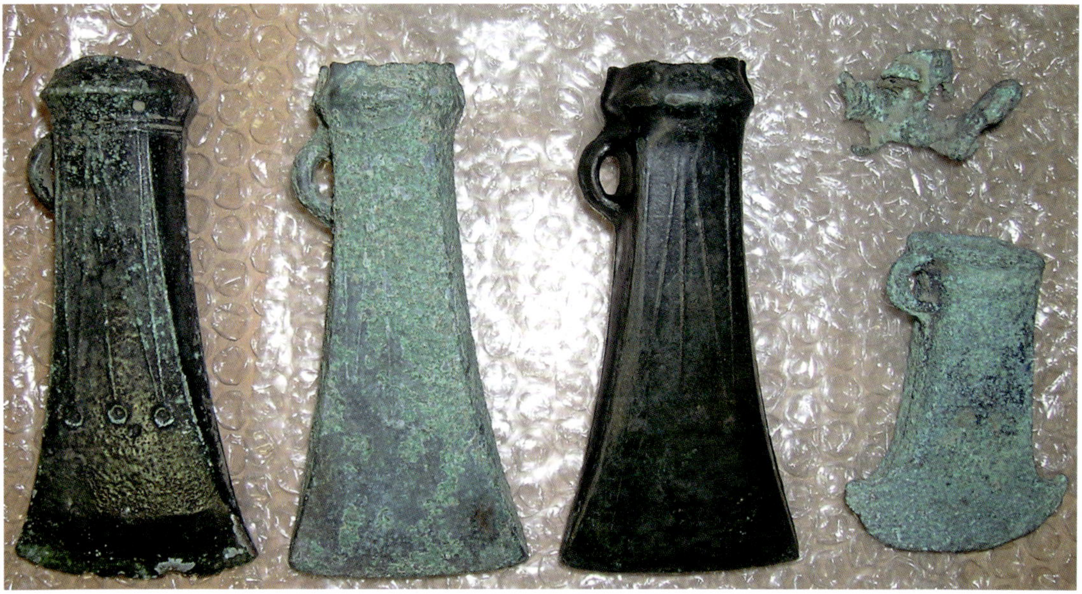

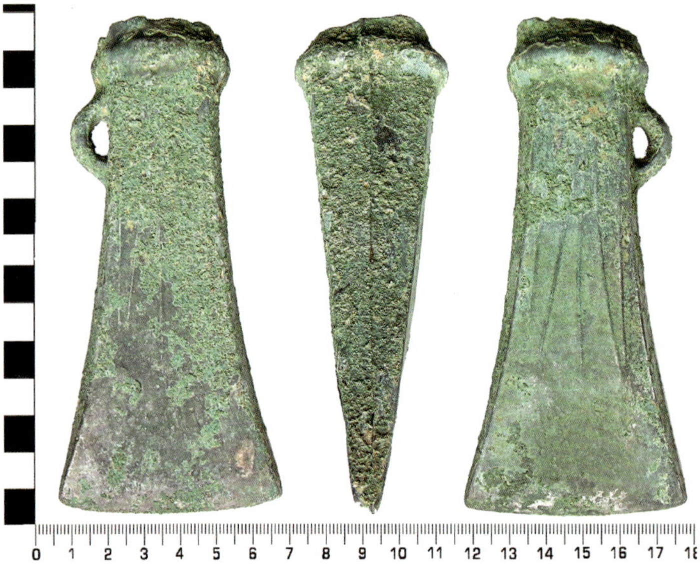

Above: LANCUM-335E04: Early Iron Age hoard from the Ulverston area (axes 1, 2 and 4); the third axe in the image was part of the Skelmore Heads hoard (see no. 12).

Left: Early Iron Age socketed axe from the Ulverston Hoard.

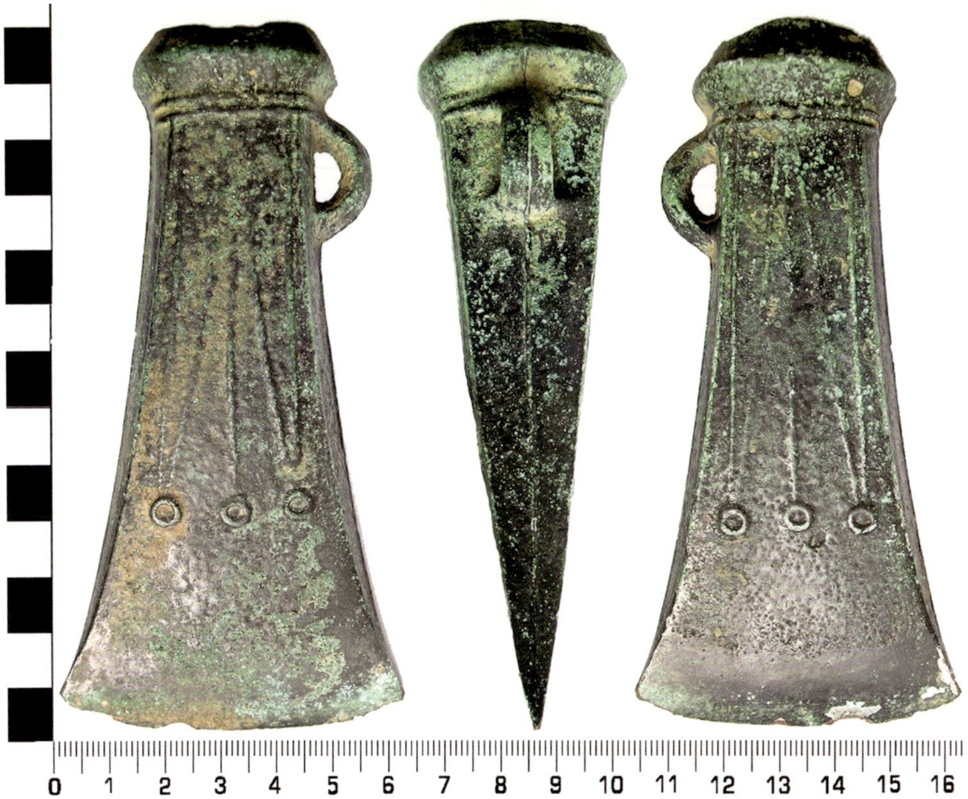

Early Iron Age socketed axe from the Ulverston Hoard.

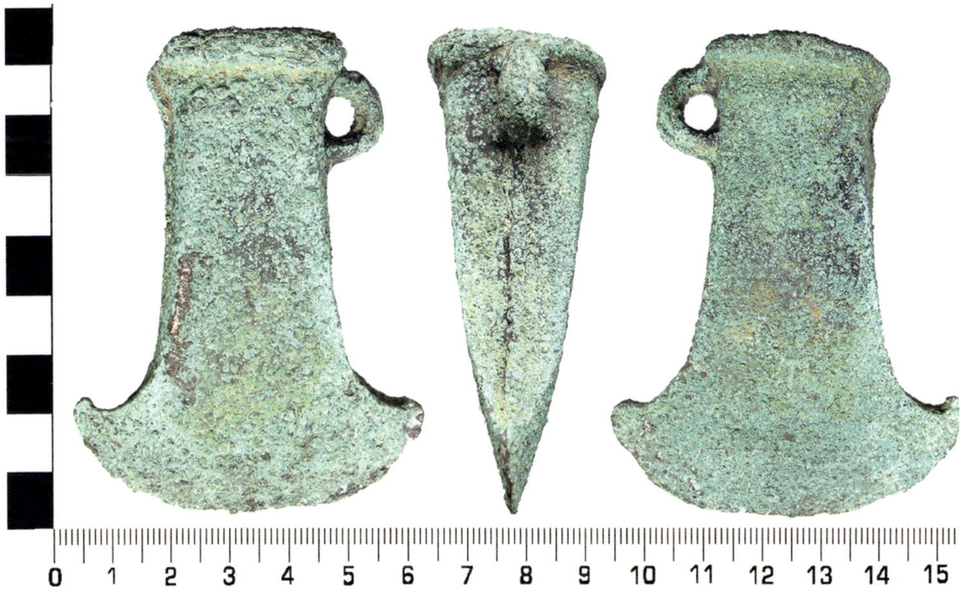

Early Iron Age socketed axe from the Ulverston Hoard.

The two decorated axes were made in the same mould, which may have been a steatite (soapstone) mould like this one from Rosskeen. The mould was also used to make at least one of the axes from the above-mentioned hoard from Skelmore Heads. British early Iron Age hoards were normally composed of large, heavy socketed axes, and it was very common for some of the axes to be deposited in as-cast condition. This means that they still had their casting flashes and were not sharpened or in any way prepared for use.

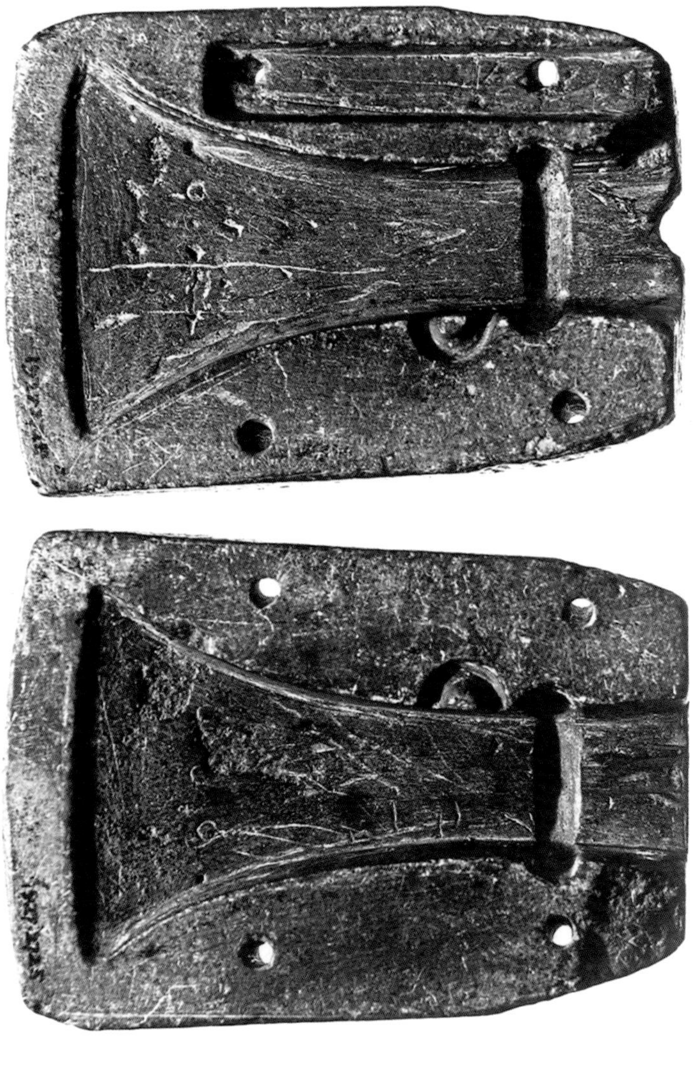

Steatite mould for Early Iron Age socketed axes from Rosskeen (Scotland).

14. Leather working knife from the Penrith area (LANCUM-1DD561)
800–600 BC
Length: 38.9 mm; Width: 31.5 mm; Thickness: 10 mm; Weight: 11.03 g

Cast copper-alloy socketed leather-working knife dating from the early Iron Age, *c.* 800–600 BC (fig. 14). The knife is composed of two parts: a rectangular socket and a crescentic blade, which are separated by a thin moulded collar. The object is complete, but the blade is very worn. It would have been more than twice its size when made; its size has been reduced by wear and re-sharpening of the blade, not by damage. Only one other leather-working knife is recorded on the database: NMS-6C4A15. There are only a few stray finds of these knives: the two on the PAS database and another from 'Staffordshire', which is in the Ashmolean Museum in Oxford. They have been found in early Iron Age hoards, however, such as the hoards from Cardiff II (Leckwith, Vale of Glamorgan), Worthing (Sussex) and possibly Salisbury (Wiltshire). Only about a dozen or so examples are known from England but, so far, there are none from Scotland or Ireland.

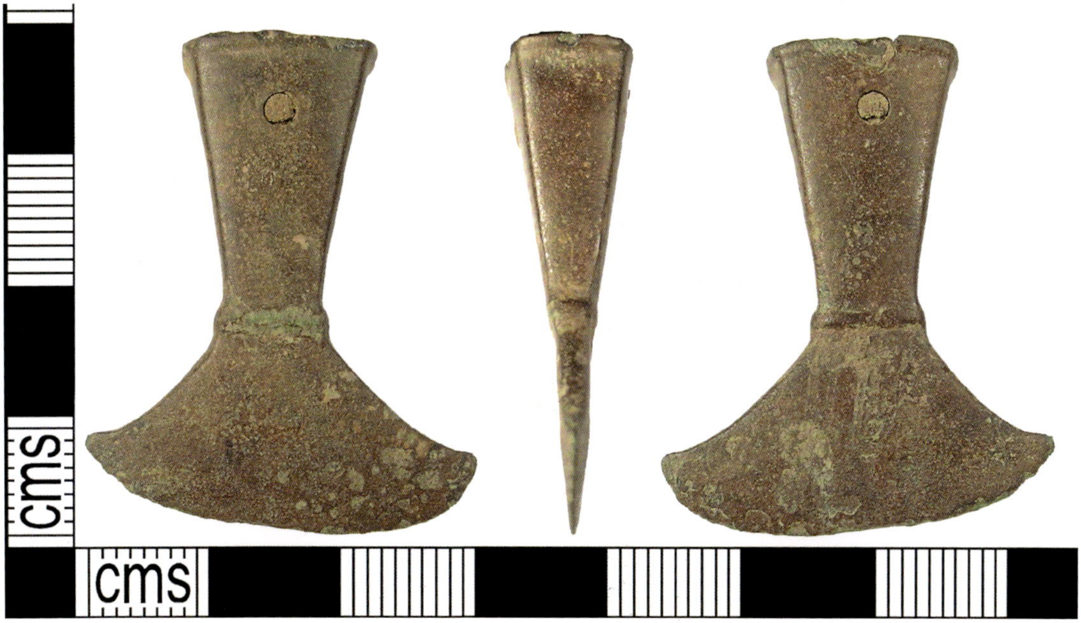

LANCUM-1DD561: Early Iron Age leather-working knife from the Penrith area.

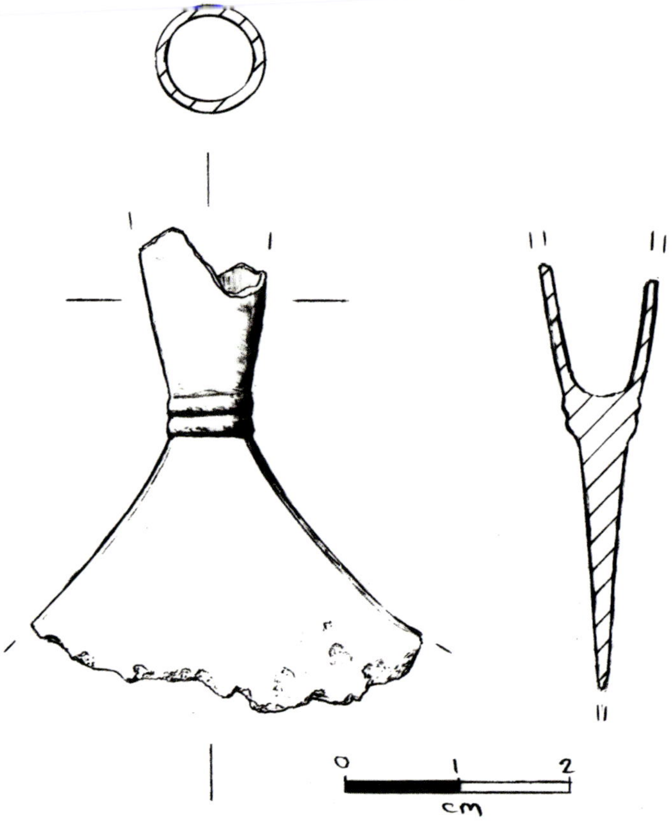

NMS-6C4A15: Early Iron Age leather-working knife from Fincham, Norfolk (drawing).

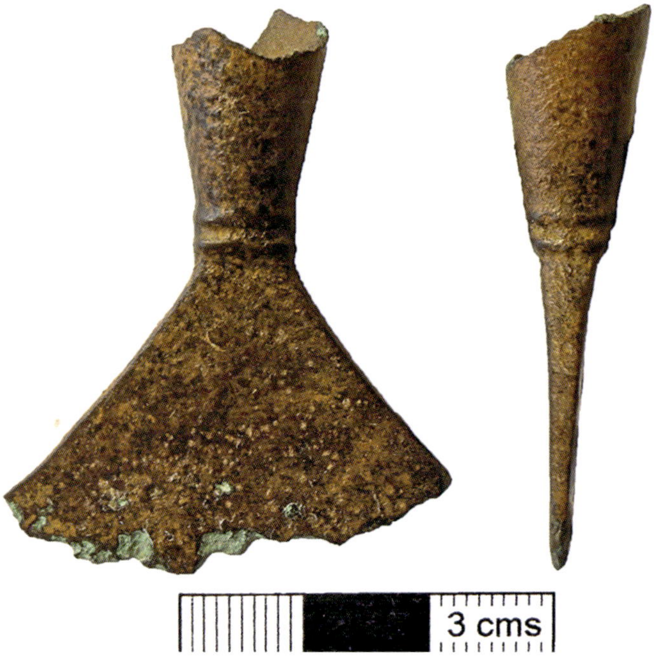

NMS-6C4A15: Early Iron Age leather-working knife from Fincham, Norfolk.

15. Gold stater from the Heversham area (LANCUM-29BDD7)
80–60 BC
Weight: 6.05 g; Diameter: 21.18 mm

British Iron Age gold stater of the north-eastern uninscribed series (often ascribed to the Corieltavi), British H or North-East Coast Type, *c.* 60–50 BC. Iron Age coins are extremely rare in Cumbria; only one other stater has been recorded on the database. This comes from the Celtic Coin Index (CCI-690169): a coin found in 1864, near Brough in the Eden Valley. However, it is very likely that both coins travelled to Cumbria in the Iron Age or Roman periods because of their metal value rather than their monetary value.

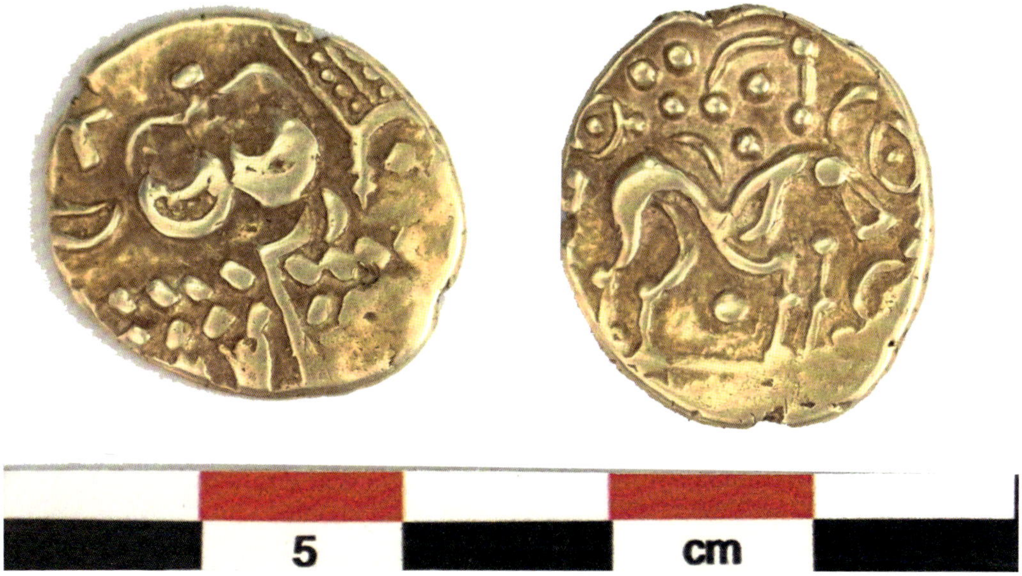

LANCUM-29BDD7: Corieltavi gold stater from the Heversham area.

16. Sword belt mount from Kents Cavern (LANCUM-30FA31)
AD 0–200
Length: 56.5 mm; Height: 13.5 mm; Width: 51.5 mm

Cast copper-alloy sword-belt fitting, dating from the late Iron Age or early Roman period, *c*. AD 0–200. The fitting is complete, undamaged and in extremely good condition. It is composed of a D-sectioned ring, with a moulded decoration at the bottom. In addition, there is a moulded knop at the bottom, just below of the mould /\-shape. Between the diagonal mouldings of the /\ is a tear- or eye-shaped moulding, and the knop below resembles one half of a late Iron Age/early Roman dumbbell mount/toggle. There are a further two complete dumbbell-shaped mounts in the centre of the ring, each of their round terminals separated by two reel-shaped mouldings and one central moulding resembling a thin melon bead. Michael Marshall (finds specialist at the Museum of London) suggests that small dumbbell-shaped mounts or toggles are very reminiscent of a series of Iron Age/Roman toggles, which are commonly found in the north of England (e.g., the example from Thwing, East Riding of Yorkshire). He argues that this design/motif is used as part of an openwork design in quite a similar fashion on a strap junction in the hoard from Middlebie, Dumfries and Galloway. Here it is combined with petal-shaped motifs, typical of boss-style metal work. This too is a late Iron Age/early Roman deposit, dating to the first or second century AD. There is no evidence to date the hoard tightly, but it is probably *c*. AD 40–160. Marshall argues further that, while these objects have previously been associated with horse/cart fittings, there is now good reason to believe that they are in fact sword-belt fittings. Two similar objects were found in close association with the late Iron Age sword from Asby Scar, Cumbria, and are interpreted as such by Ian Stead.

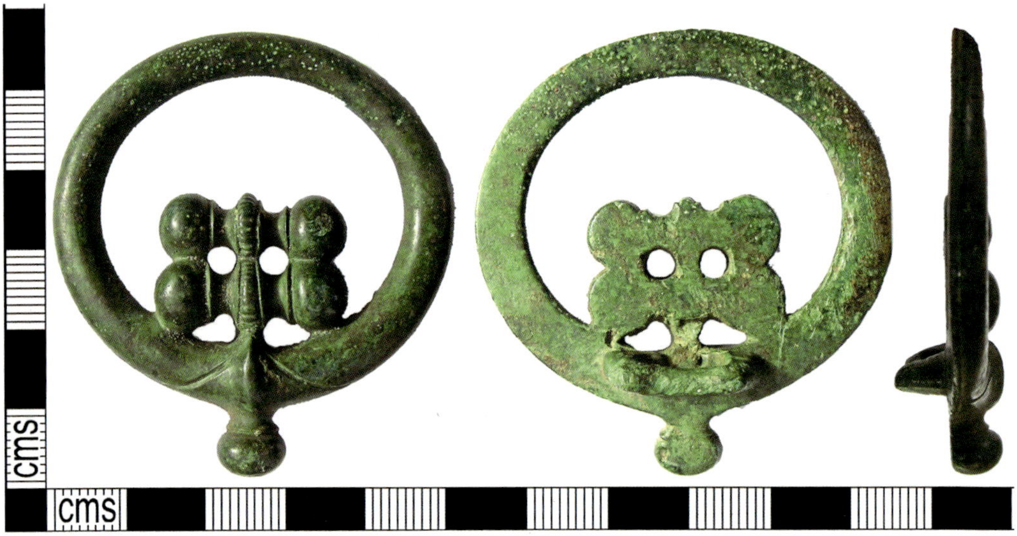

LANCUM-30FA31: Iron Age sword belt mount from Kents Bank.

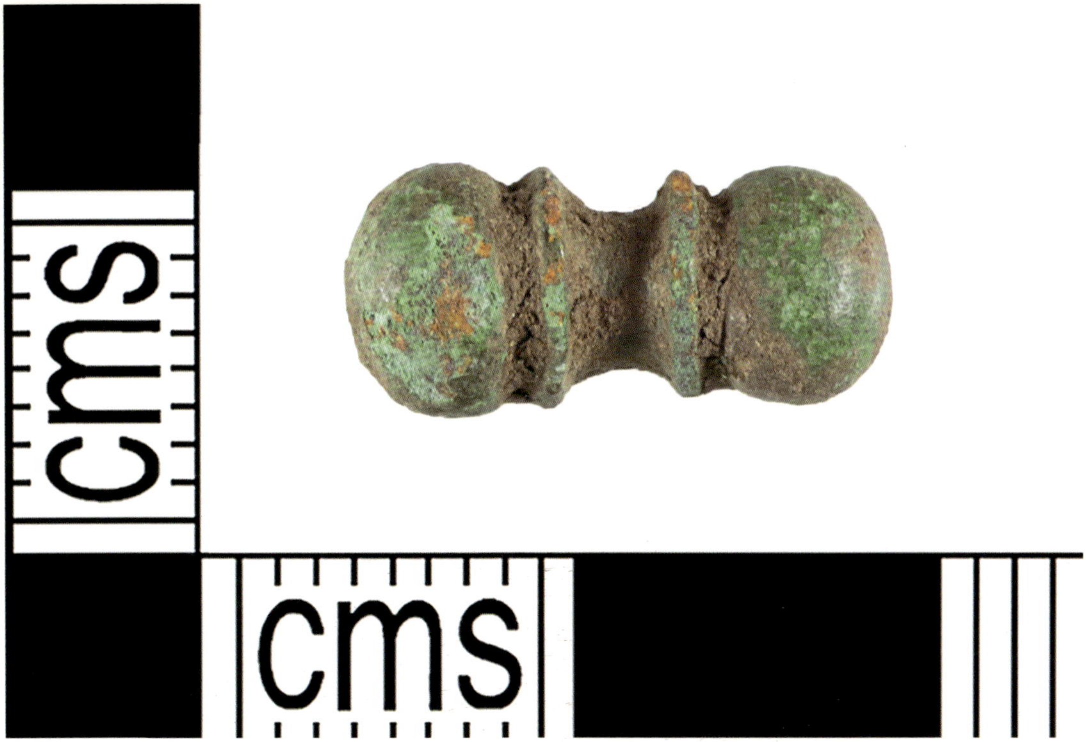

YORYM-44D65D: Toggle/dumbbell-shaped mount from Thwing, East Yorkshire.

17. Middle Iron Age brooch from the Urswick area: (LANCUM-520697)
300–200 BC
Length: 54 mm; Width: 37 mm; Thickness: 0.6 mm; Weight: 40.77 g

Very unusual cast copper-alloy brooch, dating to the late Iron Age. It is of a rare type, which is composed of a central wheel-shaped ornament with four spokes, a central raised knop and three groups of 'knops', which are moulded on to the 'wheel'. There is a little group of five knops at the foot and two little groups of four knops at the head end. Between the latter two is a small loop for attaching a chain or string with beads. The central part of the brooch is decorated with punched ring-and-dot decoration. This brooch was probably worn on a shoulder, with another one on the other and a string or chain between them. The iron pin and hinge is missing. Only very few of these brooches have been recorded on the Portable Antiquities Scheme's database, two of them are these similar examples from Lichfield (Staffordshire, WMID-C83644) and Ludlow (Shropshire, HESH-B7DED).

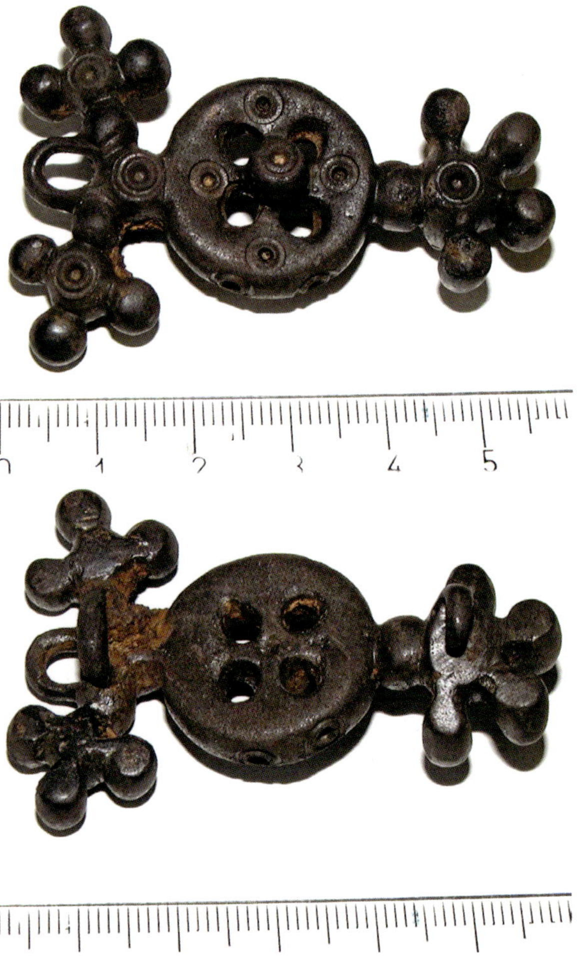

LANCUM-520697: Middle Iron Age brooch from the Urswick area.

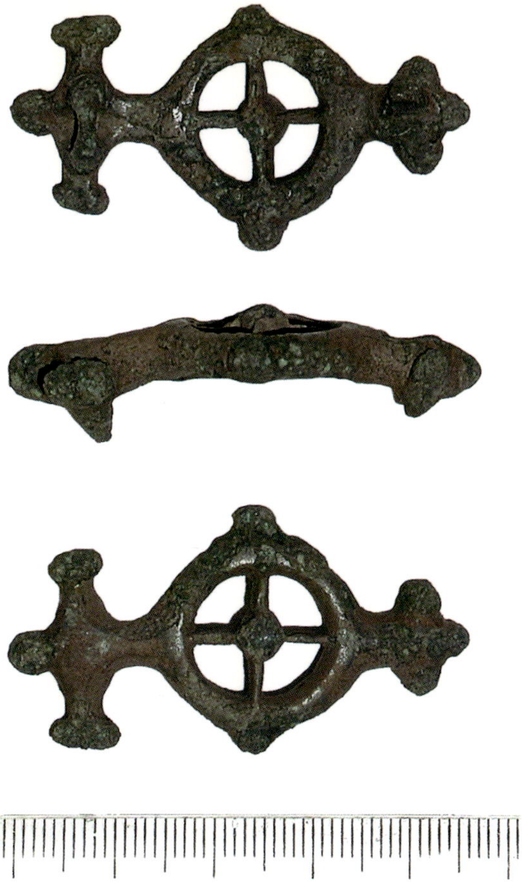

WMID-C83644: Middle Iron Age brooch from Lichfield, Staffordshire.

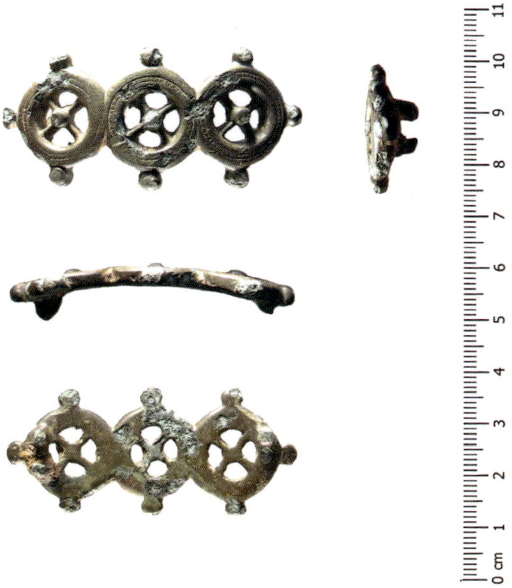

HESH-B7DED: Middle Iron Age brooch from Ludlow, Shropshire.

Chapter 4
Roman

Even though Britain was part of the Roman Empire in the first to the fourth century AD, it had never become truly Romanised to the same degree as Gaul and Spain had. This means that we find more surviving Iron Age elements in British metalwork, sculpture and pottery than we do on the Continent. Iron Age metalwork traditions survived in Roman disguise, and one of the most impressive examples is the Romano-British production of enamelled vessels and brooches, unique within the empire. For the Romans, Britain was known as the source of metal – mainly tin, silver and gold – and the local craftsmen were renowned throughout the empire for their beautifully decorated metalwork. Philostratus of Lemnos in the third century specifically referred to enamelled metalwork, reporting that it was a typical product of the people on the north-west coast of the empire, including the British Isles. Among the metalwork assemblage, certain decorated types are very characteristic for Roman Britain: enamelled and finely moulded bronze brooches, toggles, strap mounts and fasteners, which combine animals, plants and inorganic elements in sophisticated compositions (nos 26 and 30).

The Roman fort at Stanwix (Carlisle) was called Uxelodunum, and was part of Hadrian's Wall. When Hadrian's Wall was built in AD 122, it demarcated the far northern edge of the Roman Empire. The frontier itself has been established about fifty years previously, along the line between Carlisle and Corbridge on what was called the Stanegate ('stone street') in the medieval period. Recent excavations have shown that the fort at Carlisle was occupied from AD 72/3 to the early fifth century. Fortifications also extended south and west from Carlisle to Maryport, but whether or not the Cumbrian coastal fortifications extended southwards from Maryport is unknown. Coastal hoards might well point to a more extensive settlement of the coastal regions of southern Cumbria and the northern flank of Morecambe Bay, with some showing signs of considerable wealth, such as the discovery of high-value items like the silver bracelet from the Furness (no. 20). Perhaps they were derived from the retirement gratuities of Roman military or administrative personnel.

Cumbria produced a large number of Roman stray coins, most of them first- and second-century denarii and sestertii. There are few coin hoards, and only two of the larger ones remain substantially extant. The hoard from Mallerstang was found in 1926 and is now on display in Tullie House Museum & Art Gallery (Carlisle), while the hoard from Maryport was discovered in late 2011/early 2012 and is now in Senhouse Roman Museum in Maryport (no. 23). The high number of second-century coin-hoard depositions has a variety of reasons. Politically and economically, the mid-second century AD was increasingly a period of local and empire-wide uncertainty. This is well demonstrated by the nature of coin loss, particularly the evident loss from circulation of the lower denominations, and the declining quality of the coinage itself.

18. Gold aureus of Nero from Cockermouth (LANCUM-A0DD8E). Parallel 1: Gold aureus of Titus from Brampton (DUR-FF7235). Parallel 2: Gold aureus of Nero from Dearham (LANCUM-78D013)
Weight: 6.9 g; Diameter: 19 mm

A gold aureus of Nero (AD 54–68) dating from *c.* AD 64–65. It has the inscription 'NERO CAESAR AVGVSTVS' on the obverse and shows Nero's head laureate right. On the reverse, it depicts Jupiter seated left on throne, holding thunderbolt and long sceptre, surrounded by the inscription 'IVPPITER CVSTOS' (RIC (Nero), 52). Roman gold aurei are extremely rare in Cumbria and so far, only these three have been recorded on the Portable Antiquities Scheme's database. In addition to the one from Cockermouth, there is another one of the same type from Dearham, which is just north of Cockermouth, and an aureus of Titus from Brampton, east of Carlisle.

The aureus from Brampton weighs 7.3 g and has a diameter of 19.5 mm. It is an aureus, which Vespasian had struck for his son, Titus, and dated to the period AD 77–78 (Reece Period 4). The reverse inscription is COS VI and depicts Roma seated right on a shield, with birds, she-wolf and twins in the field. It was minted in Rome, Cf RIC II (ed. 2) no. 954. The second parallel, found close to Cockermouth at Dearham, is another aureus of Nero, also dating from AD 64–5. The obverse shows Nero's bust right and the inscription reads 'NERO CAESAR AVGVSTVS'; while the reverse reads 'IVPPITER CVSTOS', depicting Jupiter enthroned left, holding thunderbolt and sceptre (RIC 52; BMC 67). Its diameter is 17 mm and the weight is 7.39 g.

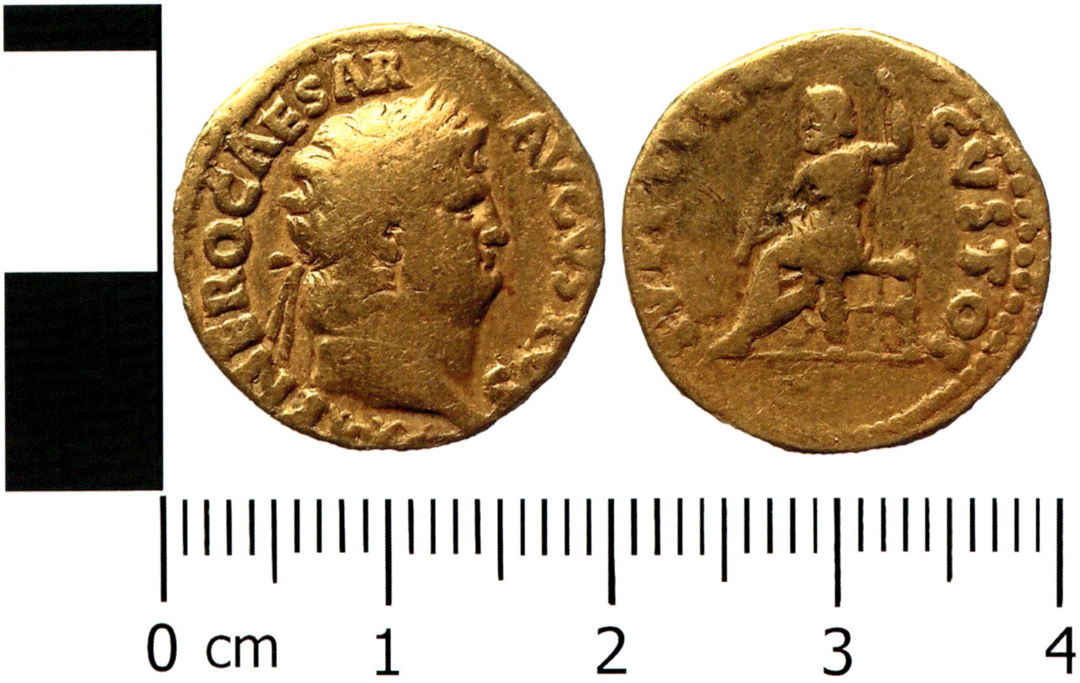

LANCUM-A0DD8E: Gold aureus of Nero from Cockermouth.

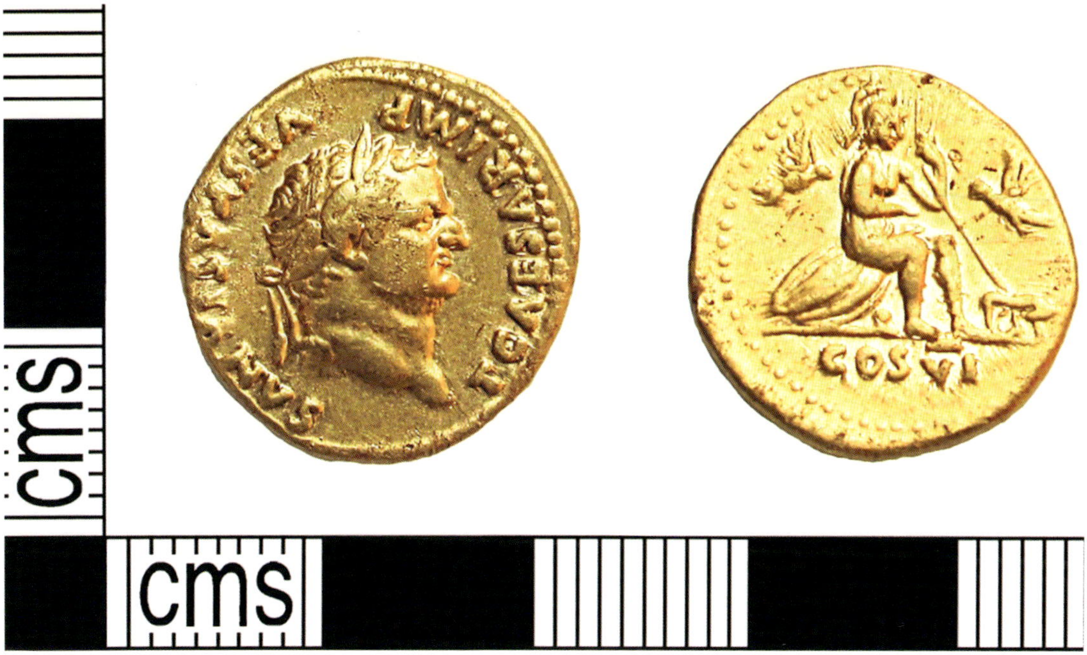

DUR-FF7235: Gold aureus of Titus from Brampton.

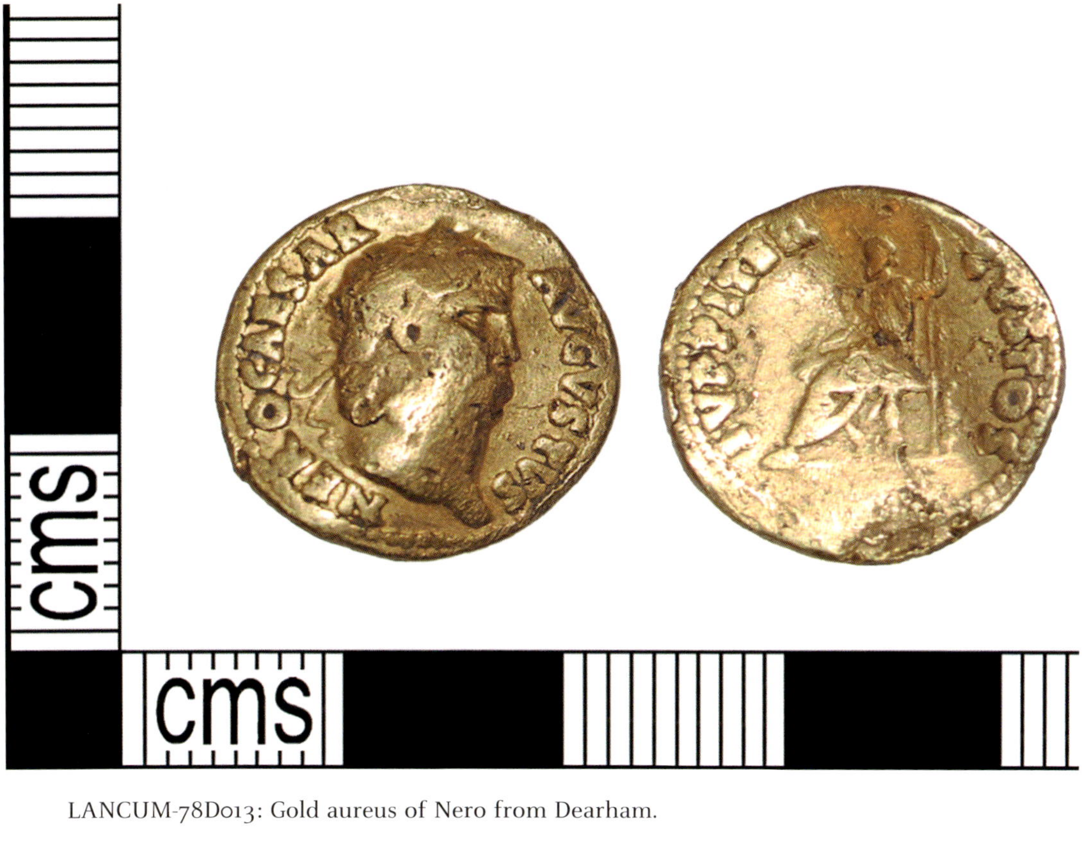

LANCUM-78D013: Gold aureus of Nero from Dearham.

19. The Crosby Garrett Helmet (LANCUM-E48D73). Parallel (LANCUM-C840D2)
Height: 407 mm

An extremely fine, near-complete, copper-alloy two-piece Roman cavalry sports helmet, dating from the late first to the mid-third century AD. The helmet consists of a face mask and a head piece with a griffin figurine crest attachment. The helmet was found in thirty-three fragments, with thirty-four smaller fragments found in association. Many of the fragments were found to join and the restored helmet is now around 90 per cent complete.

Ralph Jackson from the British Museum and Sally Worrell, the Portable Antiquities Scheme's Finds Advisor for Roman finds, suggest that the face mask depicts an idealised youthful male face, with luxuriant curly hair in three rows, the first of which extends to the mid-point of the full cheeks. The fine eyebrows are indicated by short diagonal engraved strokes, the eyelids are shown and both eyes are depicted with a pierced ring in the centre of the eye-holes to represent the iris. Traces of the reserved white metal coating are visible on the face, but it is likely that the hair and helmet would have appeared in bright natural bronze. The nostrils are pierced and the full lips slightly parted.

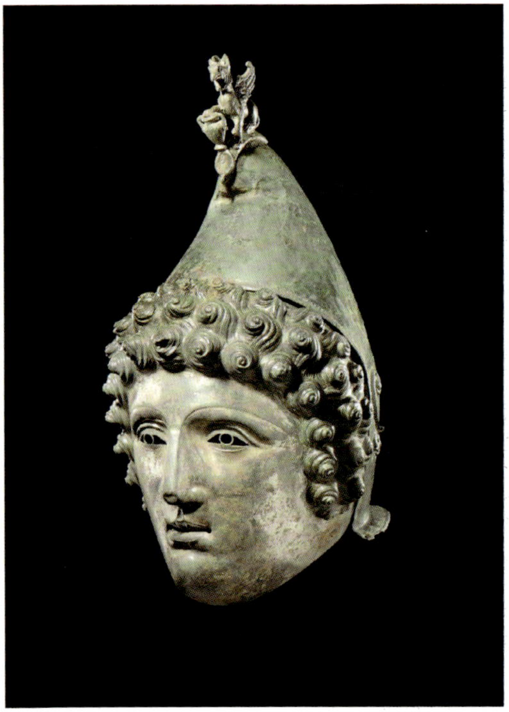

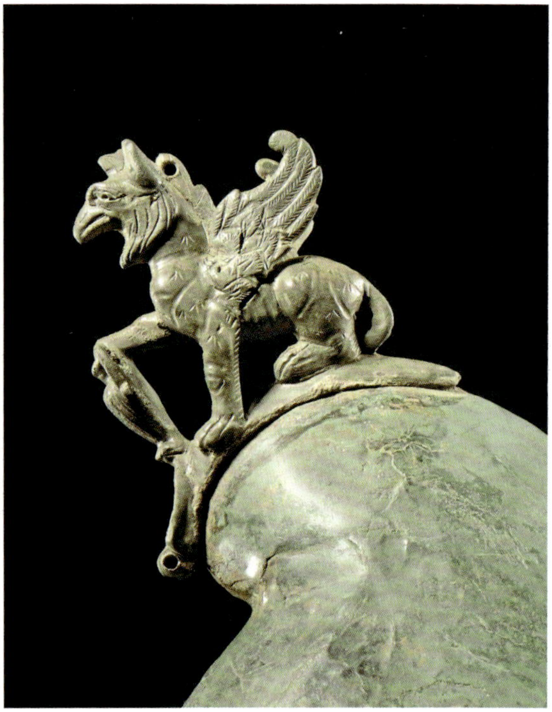

Above left:LANCUM-E48D73: The Crosby Garrett Helmet (after conservation). (Copyright Christie's)

Above right: LANCUM-E48D73: The griffin crest. (Copyright Christie's)

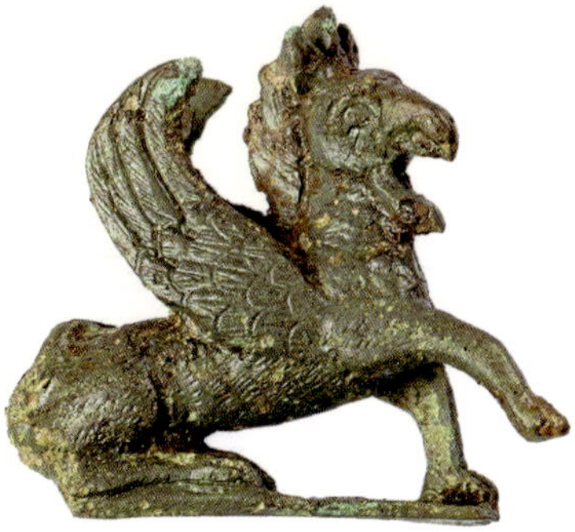

Small griffin mount from Vindolanda. (Copyright Vindolanda Trust)

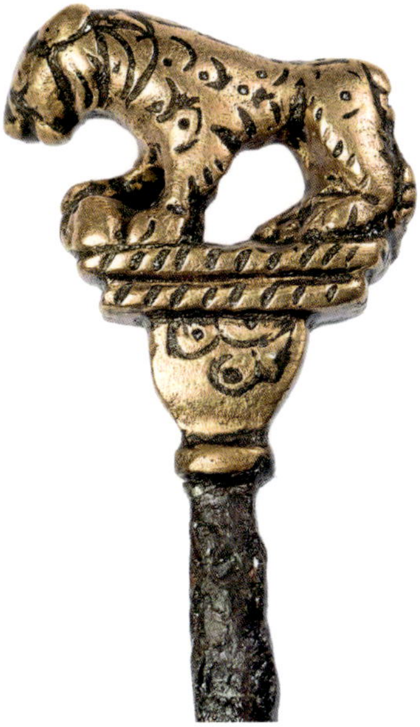

Pointer with leopard terminal found at Vindolanda. (Copyright Vindolanda Trust)

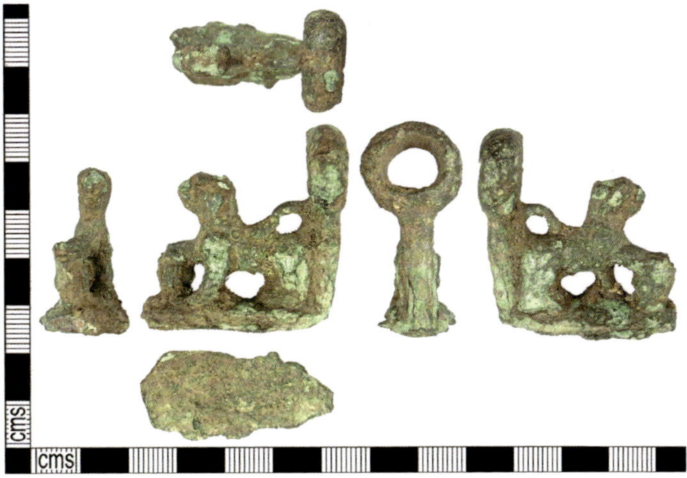

LANCUM-C840D2: Small leopard mount from Carlisle.

Originally the mask would have hinged at the centre of the brow, within the curly hair. At the neck, it was fastened by a leather strap, which would have been secured by its eyeleted ends to an iron strap on the jawline on each side of the mask, with slight remains of iron corrosion surviving. The survival of the headpiece in its Phrygian form is exceptional, with a crest attachment in the form of a winged griffin, its right paw raised and resting on an amphora. At the back of the head, a single row of curls can be seen below a raised ridge.

The image of griffin or a large feline sat on his hind legs, with one of the front paws resting on, for example, an amphora is well documented from other findspots along Hadrian's Wall. An exceptionally good parallel was discovered at the fort of Vindolanda, which appears to be a small griffin sat on a flat pedestal, with one paw raised. It is uncertain if his paw was resting on a vessel or perhaps on a severed human head, like on the little leopard furniture mount from Carlisle and a second example from Vindolanda, which has been identified as a pointer terminal. The leopard mount from Carlisle is 39.5 mm long, 40.5 mm high and weighs 42.68 g, recorded as LANCUM-C840D2. While the find from Vindolanda appears to be the terminal of a pointer, the small mount from Carlisle was probably a furniture mount. It is 39.5 mm long, 40.5 mm high and weighs 42.68 g, recorded as LANCUM-C840D2. It is a little leopard walking or standing on an oval/eye-shaped platform with a loop behind. Its front right leg is raised, the paw resting on a severed human head. The other three feet stand firmly on the ground. The animal stands proudly, with its head erect, and the tail curled forward and resting on the back. The animal is clearly depicted as feline, and some of the moulded leopard spots are still clearly visible on the flanks of the animal's body. The facial features, eyes, snout and ears are finely moulded, as are the hair and facial features of the severed human head. The reverse and bottom of the mount are not as finely moulded, and it is more than likely that these surfaces rested against a wooden mount/box/plank or other object. The inside of the loop at the top looks worn, and it may have held one end of a chain or rope.

The image of the leopard was widely used in the Roman period, but these objects are comparatively rare in Britain: there are images of leopards on Samian ware vessels, felines as knife guards, hilts or grips and there are leopard brooches. Generally, however, the latter have a more continental distribution and there are only three recorded on the PAS database: one from Shalfleet parish, Isle of Wight (IOW-1402E8), Little Waltham parish, Essex (CAM-925392), and Chilton in Oxfordshire (SUR-1460B5).

The image of the severed head is also not an usual one in the Roman period. It is not so much used in classical Roman imagery, but rather influenced by provincial art. A Roman soldier (who was, however, from the German tribe of the Treveri) is depicted on a tombstone from Lancaster: he is riding a horse, with a sword and a severed head of his opponent in his hands, while his opponent's headless body is still kneeling below him. The tradition of beheading opponents was attributed to Celtic or Germanic tribes, and it was thought that only that would 'really' kill a person. It is a very powerful image.

20. The Furness bracelet (PAS-A7DC11)
AD 100–300
Length: 80 mm; Width: 61 mm; Weight: 58.2 g; Diameter: 26.8 mm

A Roman silver bracelet, now broken in two, with a twisted hoop and hinged bezel.

The distorted elliptical hoop comprises a fine and evenly twisted, tightly spiralled tube made from circular-sectioned silver wire. Quite heavy wear is visible on both sides of the hoop. What appears to be the central core, around which the wire was spiralled, is visible under magnification in those places where distortion has slightly 'opened' the twisted strands, but its composition is uncertain. Each terminal is enclosed in a tubular collar, which is decorated with an applied central meander filigree wire, flanked by a double-ring edge-moulding. The rectangular opening in their broken end once secured the hinged ends of the now-separate bezel. There is recent damage to the side of the hoop and to the side of one terminal. Further damage to the terminals and the distortion of the hoop may be ancient.

The large circular bezel, a hollow box construction of silver sheet, has a plain back and sides. Its ornate upper face comprises an outer basal zone of herringbone pattern, formed from three concentric circles of twisted wire, and a central, raised open dome with ribbed side and stepped, apparently rubbed-over, setting. The oval gem, seemingly of translucent orange-red colour, has dropped out of position to the base of the box-setting, presumably as a result of the deterioration and loss of an original organic packing. Engraved into its lightly convex surface is the image of a seated Jupiter, with wreath and full-length drapery, holding a sceptre in his left hand. In his extended right hand, he holds a patera above a stylised flaming altar.

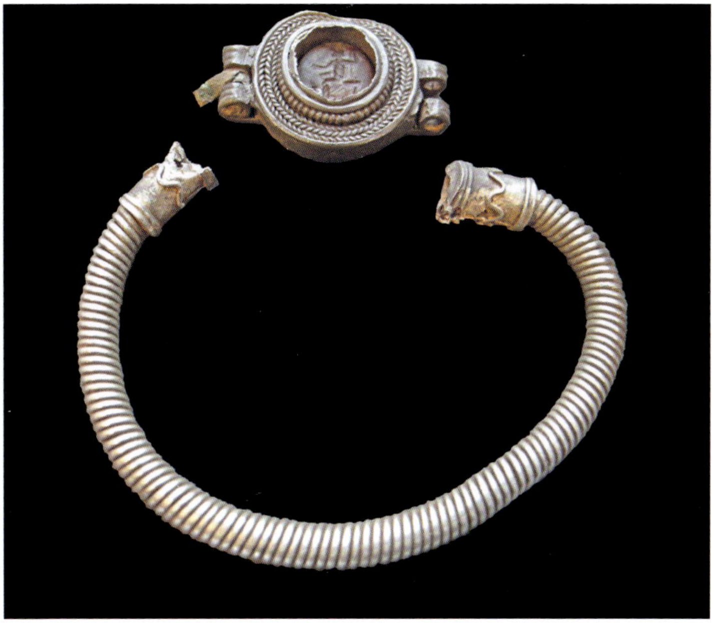

PAS-A7DC11:
The Furness bracelet.

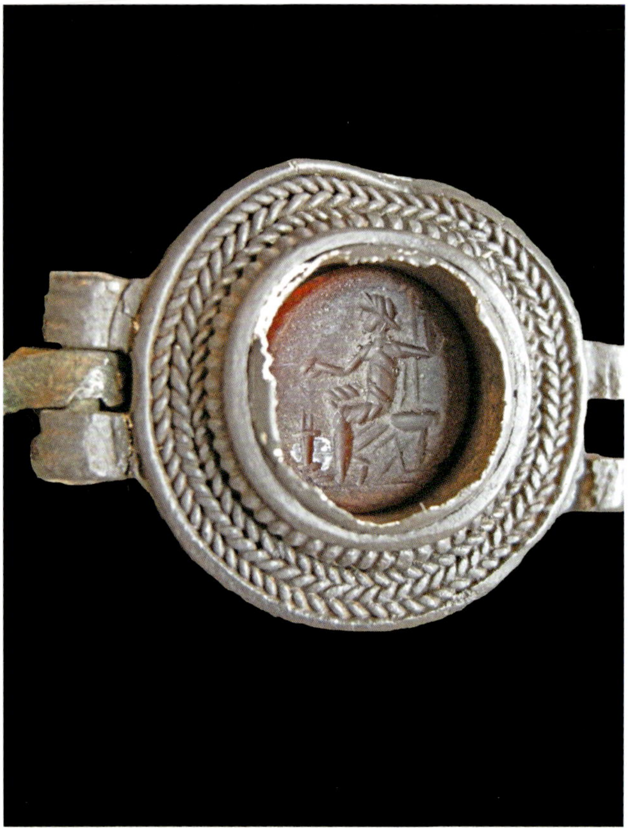

PAS-A7DC11: The Furness bracelet: detail of the bezel.

The bezel was fastened to the hoop by means of a pair of silver strips, soldered to the back of the bezel. Their rolled terminals form a pair of lugs at either side of the bezel. One pair, which acted as a hinge, retains a fixed axis bar, at the centre of which is the remains of a simple looped hinge-tag – the other end of this was originally fixed (probably soldered) into one of the hoop terminals. The other pair of lugs, now empty, would have held some form of removable locking pin, which passed through the lugs and a central loop projecting from the other hoop terminal. The back plate of the bezel and the rim of the setting have both suffered recent damage.

21. Fragment from a Roman glass vessel from the Silloth area (LANCUM-91E341)
AD 150–225
Length: 31 mm; Width: 20.5 mm; Thickness: 3 mm; Weight: 4.23 g

Two rim-fragments of a glass vessel dating from the Roman period, *c.* AD 150–225. The fragments join to form a small triangular sherd of glass from the rim of the vessel, which was probably a cylindrical cup with fire-rounded rim and double-base ring. Glass cups of this type were normally made from colourless or greenish glass, occasionally with a blueish-green tinge. On the inside, this glass fragment is plain, but the outside has been decorated with a painted ornament composed of a dotted border (alternating blue and red dots), with the remains of a head and sword below. The head is helmeted, and behind it is what appears to be a sword, held horizontally over the shoulder as if to carry out a blow. The helmet was painted in yellow and red; the face (or presumably face mask) is light blue, with a black outline and black dot for an eye. The sword hand or hilt is yellow, while the blade is light blue with a black outline on the underside. The figure was probably a gladiator and may have come from the same workshop from which the almost complete painted glass vessel from Vindolanda came. The glass vessel from Vindolanda has been attributed to workshops in Germany. There are also three rim-fragments, decorated with painted dots from Birdoswald, but more colours were used here (white, pale green, deep pink, pale yellow and pale blue). Cups of this kind come from Roman sites in Denmark and Germany, but also from Britain, where they have been found mainly from sites close to the northern frontier.

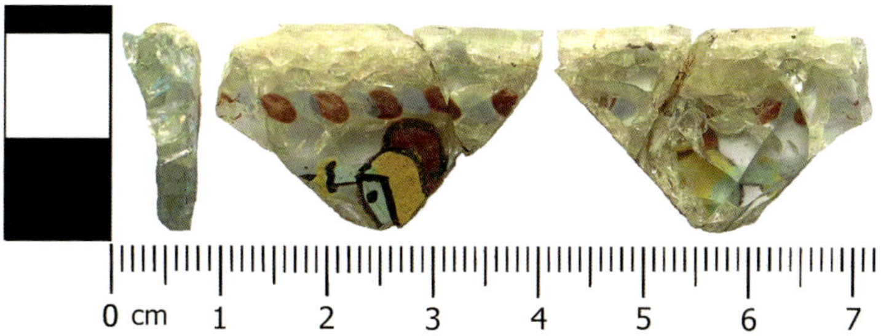

LANCUM-91E341: Fragment of a painted glass cup.

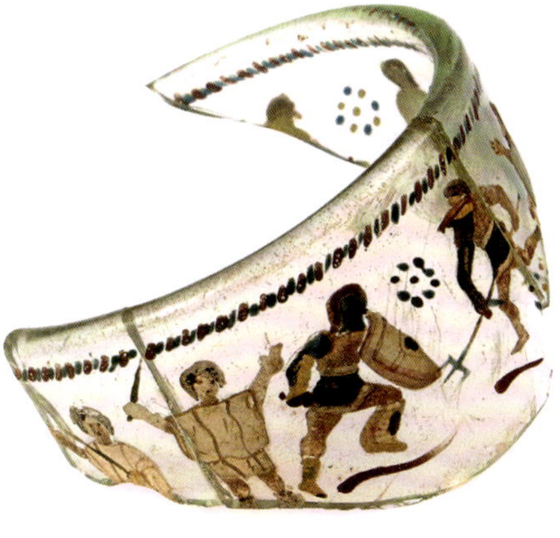

Almost complete painted glass cup from Vindolanda. (Vindolanda Trust)

22. Minerva intaglio (LANCUM-306098)

AD 100–200

Length: 14 mm; Width: 12 mm; Thickness: 4 mm; Weight: 0.67 g

Roman carnelian intaglio, depicting the goddess Minerva facing left. Probably from a ring. The sides are bevelled, the two main surfaces are convex and the reverse is plain. It dates from the late first to the second century AD.

The intaglio represents the helmeted Roman goddess of war, Minerva, with a spear and shield and, holding onto her hand, a small winged Victory. This is a type that was favoured by the military community, as opposed to other depictions of Minerva that do not include the Victory.

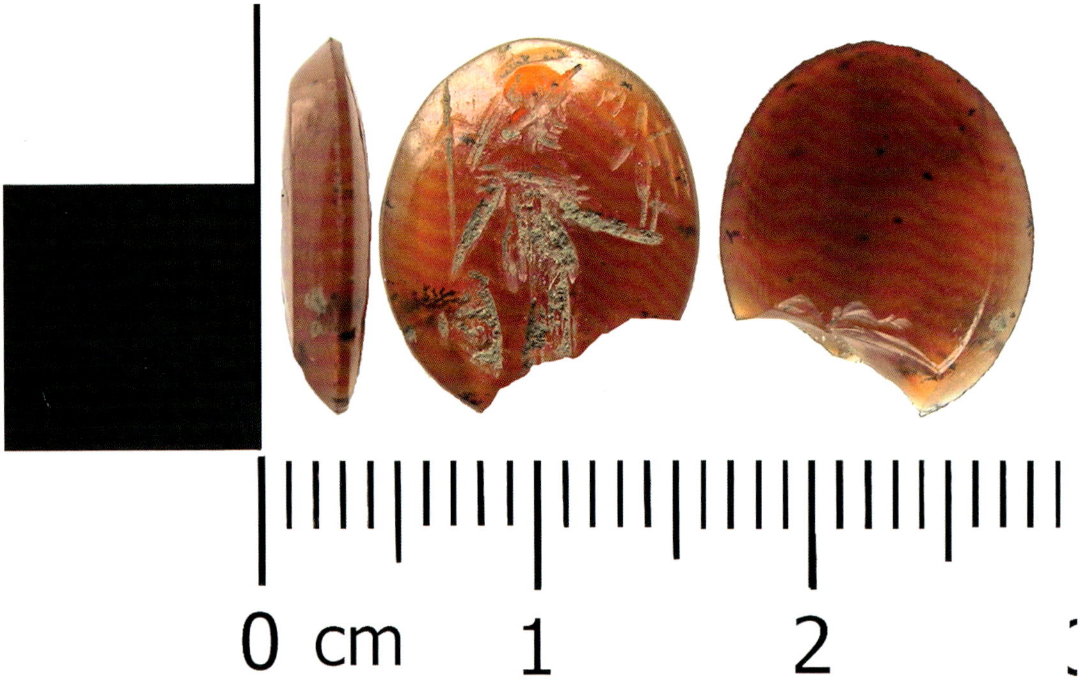

LANCUM-306098: Intaglio displaying the Roman goddess Minerva.

23. The Maryport Hoard (LANCUM-E88322)
Deposited before AD 161.
143 AR denarii and 1 AE sestertius AD 161; BM ref.: 2012 T529

This deposit consists of 143 denarii, which range in date from the late Republic to the early years of the reign of Marcus Aurelius (32 BC – *c.* AD 161); the coins are preserved in a generally good condition.

The coins range from the legionary denarii of Marc Antony to a commemorative issue for Antoninus Pius, and include two coins of Faustina II struck during the reign of Marcus. The absence of coins issued for Marcus Aurelius and Lucius Verus as emperors suggests that the closing date should be placed in, or only a little after, AD 161. In terms of the history of the northern frontier in Britain, this date coincides, of course, with the process of abandonment of the Antonine Wall and the full reoccupation of Hadrian's Wall.

However, while it might be tempting to associate this coin find, and indeed others that terminated in the Antonine period, with an episode of uncertainty on the frontier, or with a putative rebellion among the tribe of the Brigantes, it might be equally appropriate to see it simply as a savings hoard, which was left un-retrieved for natural reasons. Not only this, but it should also be borne in mind that the mid-second century AD was a period of considerable uncertainty for economic and financial (as well as for military and political) reasons. Earlier denarii may well have been hoarded at a time when the current silver coinage was being increasingly alloyed with other metals – and thus decreasing in public confidence. Similar fears, caused by a range of uncertainties, might also have accounted for an urge to use such coins as offerings to the gods, in the hope of warding off an impending doom.

A similar hoard was found close to Oswestry (Shropshire, HESH-240286).

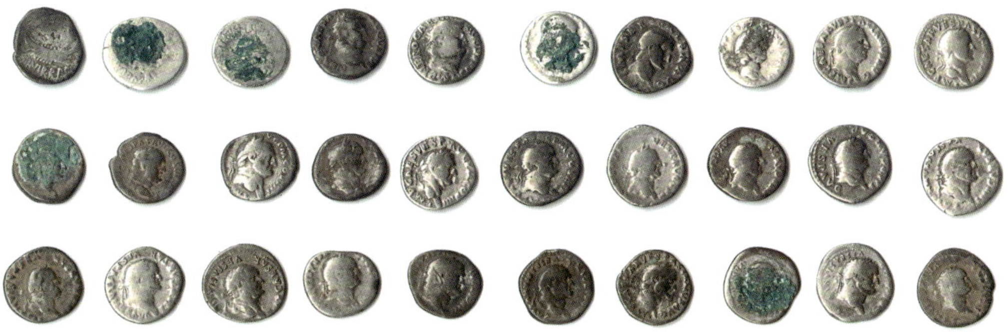

LANCUM-E88322: Fifteen Coins from the Maryport Roman coin hoard (coin obverses).

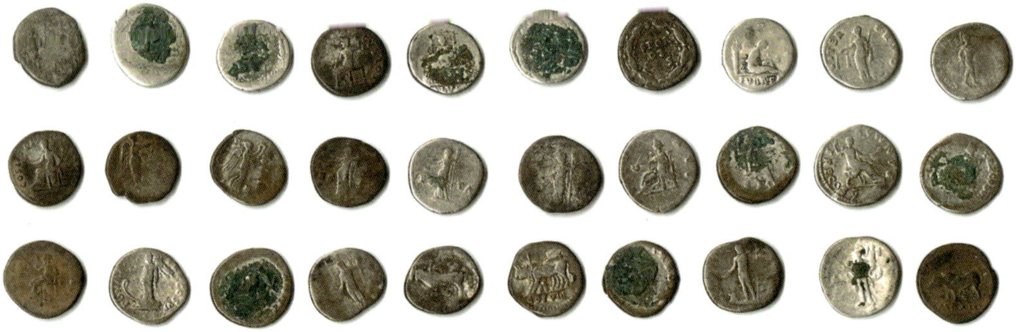

LANCUM-E88322: Fifteen Coins from the Maryport Roman coin hoard (coin reverses).

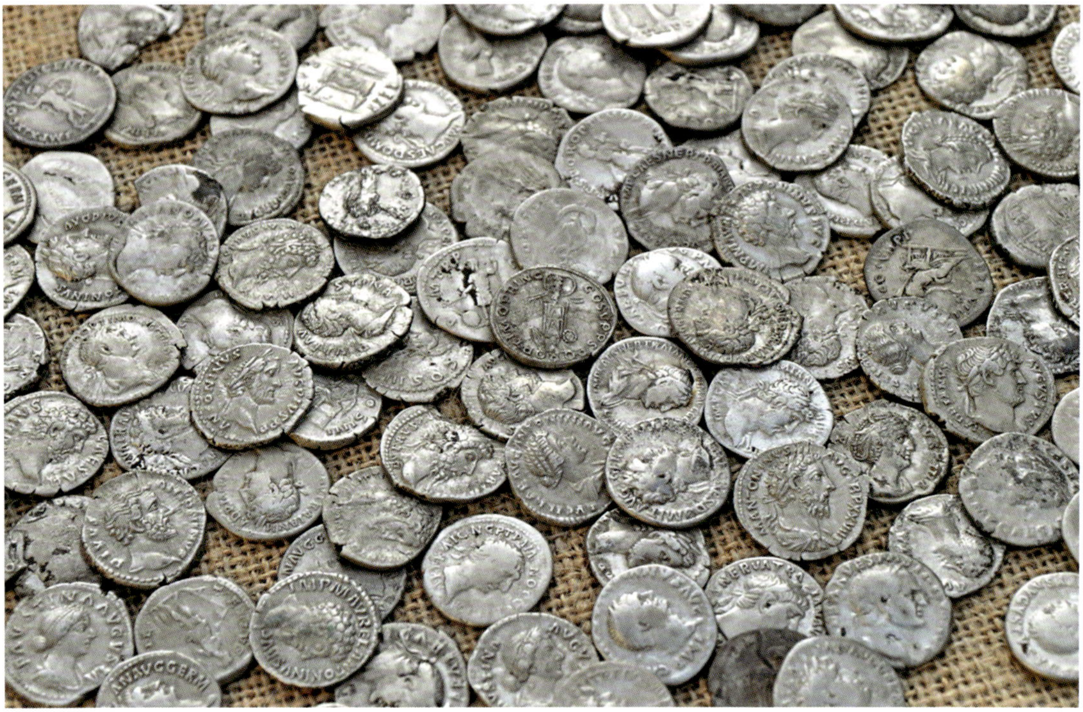

HESH-240286: Roman coin hoard from Old Oswestry, Shropshire.

24. Roman iron knife and scabbard mount from the Dalton-in-Furness area (LANCUM-1B1C8A)

AD 43–200

A Roman iron knife blade and a cast copper-alloy scabbard fitting, found together. The knife measures 125 mm in length, 16.5 mm in width and 6 mm in thickness, and weighs 33.24 g. The scabbard fitting, which came from the top of the sheath, measures 35 mm × 11.5 mm × 8 mm, and the metal is around 1.2 mm thick. It weighs 10.07 g.

This type of knife is long-lived, but the scabbard mount probably dates from the earlier Roman period – that is, the first or second century AD. The knife was tanged with a probably symmetrical, leaf-shaped blade, and a tang that the wooden handle was mounted on. The scabbard fitting was made from cast copper alloy and would have been mounted on the leather sheath, at the mouth opening. It seems to be undecorated, except for moulded horizontal grooves along the long, straight edges. The mount is a pointed oval in plan. In profile, each side of the lower edge is double-arched to give a biconcave shape, the centre portion between the arches being slightly longer than the outer ends. A very similar mount from York was recorded under SWYOR-4F9DC5.

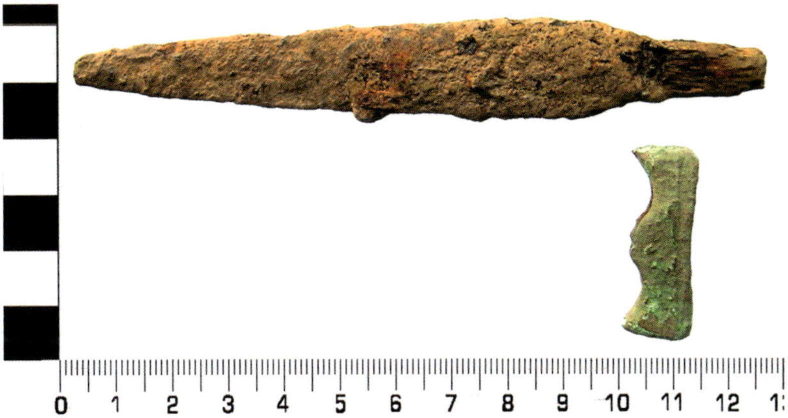

LANCUM-1B1C8A: Roman iron knife and scabbard mount from the Dalton-in-Furness area.

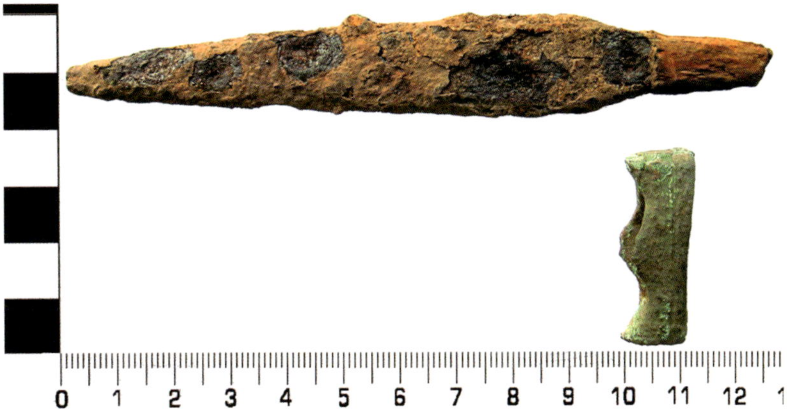

LANCUM-1B1C8A: Roman iron knife and scabbard mount from the Dalton-in-Furness area.

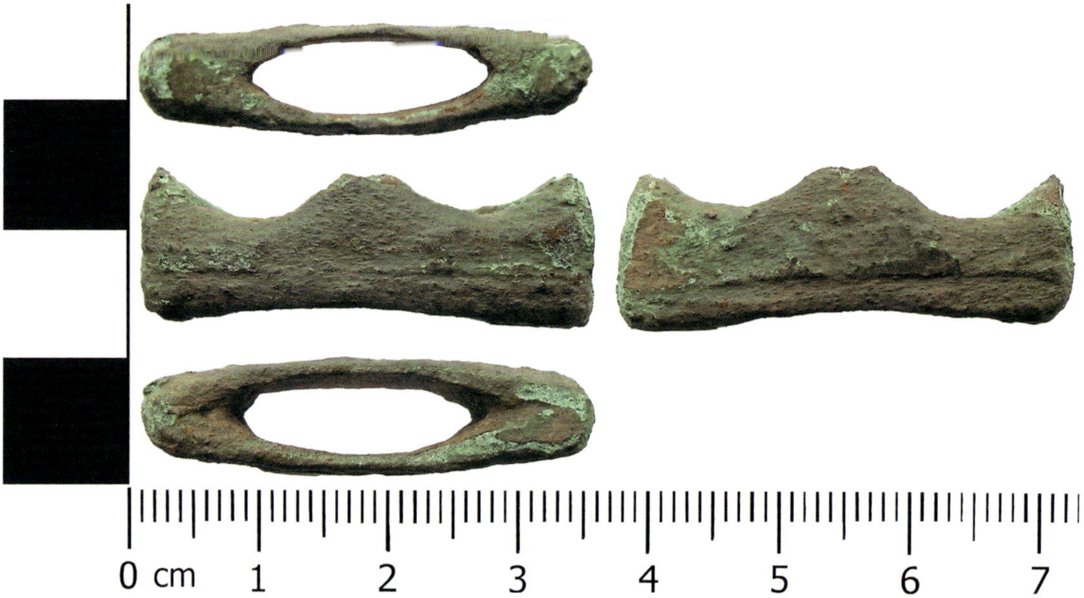

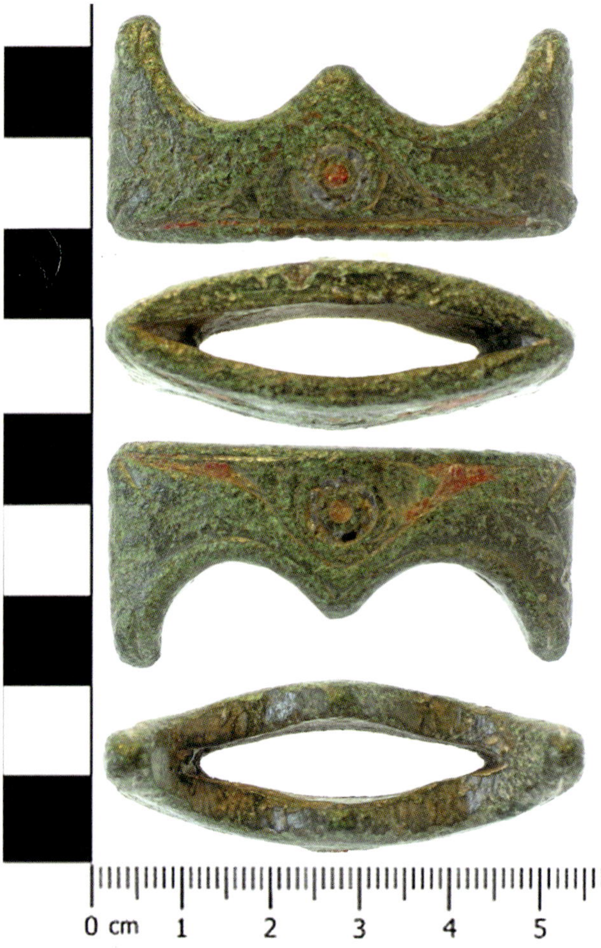

Above: LANCUM-1B1C8A: Roman bronze scabbard mount from the Dalton-in-Furness area.

Left: SWYOR-4F9DC5: Roman bronze scabbard mount from York.

25. Satyr vessel mount from the Heversham area (LANCUM-1747E5)
AD 100–300
Length: 46.1 mm; Width: 42.9 mm; Thickness: 18 mm; Weight: 45.85 g

Cast copper-alloy vessel mount in the shape of a satyr, dating from the Roman period, *c.* AD 43–410. The mount is complete and undamaged, showing a satyr's bust (chest, shoulders and head) on the obverse, and a hollow, solder-filled reverse. The bust has a youthful face with long, wavy hair, parted in the centre of the head. The friendly-looking face has moulded eyes, eyebrows, nose and a smiling mouth. There are also two small, curled-up, incipient horns on the satyr's forehead. The mount would have ornamented an item of furniture, or a box or small chest. Martin Henig suggests that quite a lot of these mounts come in the shapes of satyrs, maenads, Bacchus or Ariadne, who are beneficent and saving powers of nature.

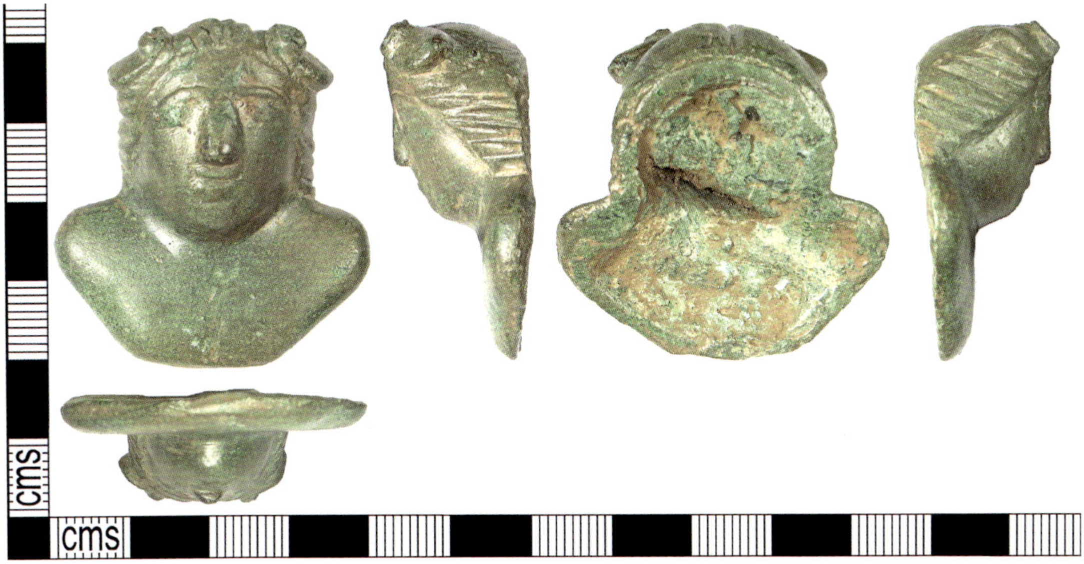

LANCUM-1747E5: Satyr vessel mount from the Heversham area.

26. Roman disc brooch from the Urswick area (LANCUM-563412)
AD 100–250
Length: 32.5 mm; Thickness: 1 mm; Weight: 7.32 g; Diameter: 19 mm

Enamelled cast copper-alloy disc brooch, with four lugs dating from *c.* AD 100–250. The brooch is complete with hinge, foot and pin on the reverse. It is in very good condition. It has four lugs (top, bottom, left and right), two of which are perforated. The brooch is plain on the back and decorated with enamelled decoration on the obverse. The enamel was applied to small cells of rectangular and tear/petal shape. The enamel used was red, turquoise, blue and yellow. The centre and two of the trapezoidal cells were decorated with dark-blue enamel, the other two with turquoise enamel, while the petals were yellow. The background and inner circle were decorated with red enamel. Enamel is rarely preserved on Roman finds from Cumbria, but there are parallels from Arnside (LANCUM-A5A195 and LANCUM-5914D5) and Longtown (LANCUM-1AB886).

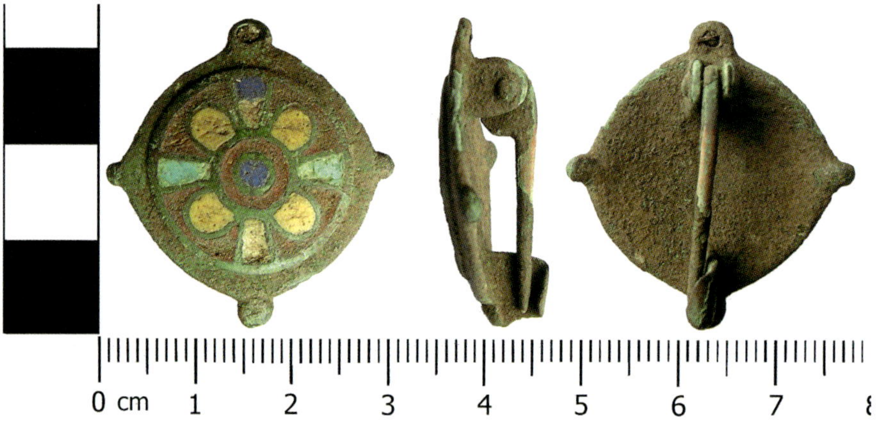

LANCUM-563412: Roman disc brooch from the Urswick area.

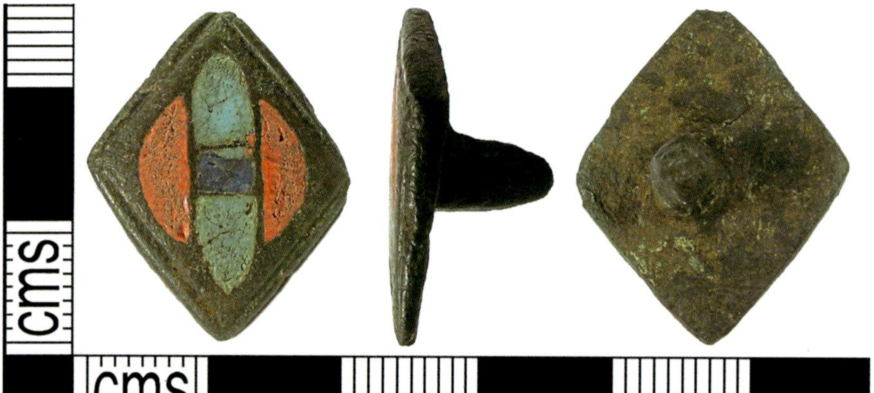

LANCUM-5914D5: Enamelled Roman stud from Arnside.

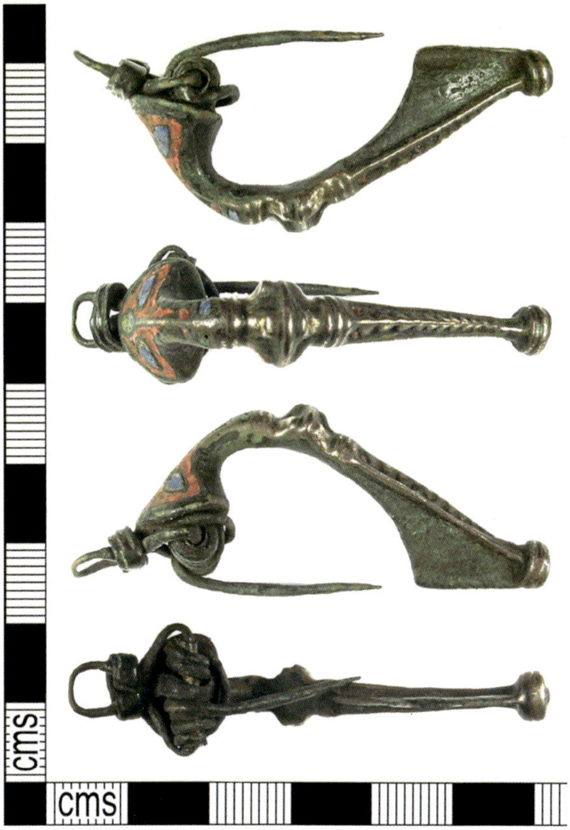

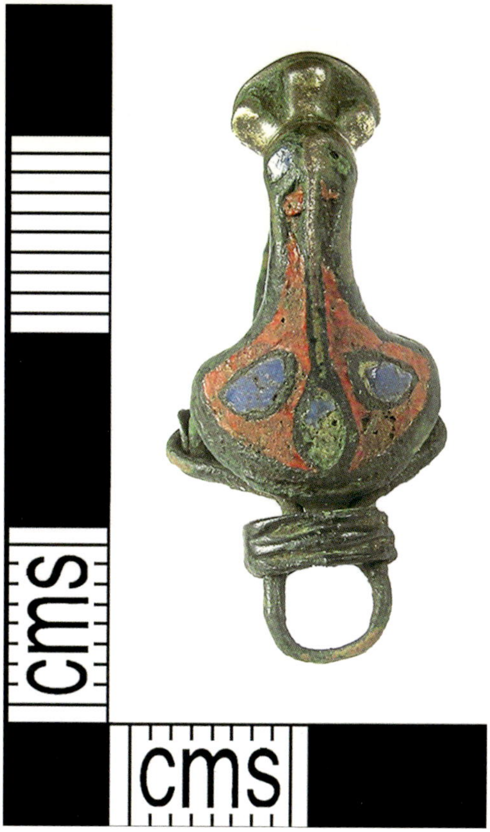

Above left: LANCUM-A5A195: Enamelled Roman trumpet brooch from Arnside.

Above right: LANCUM-A5A195: Enamelled Roman trumpet brooch from Arnside (close-up).

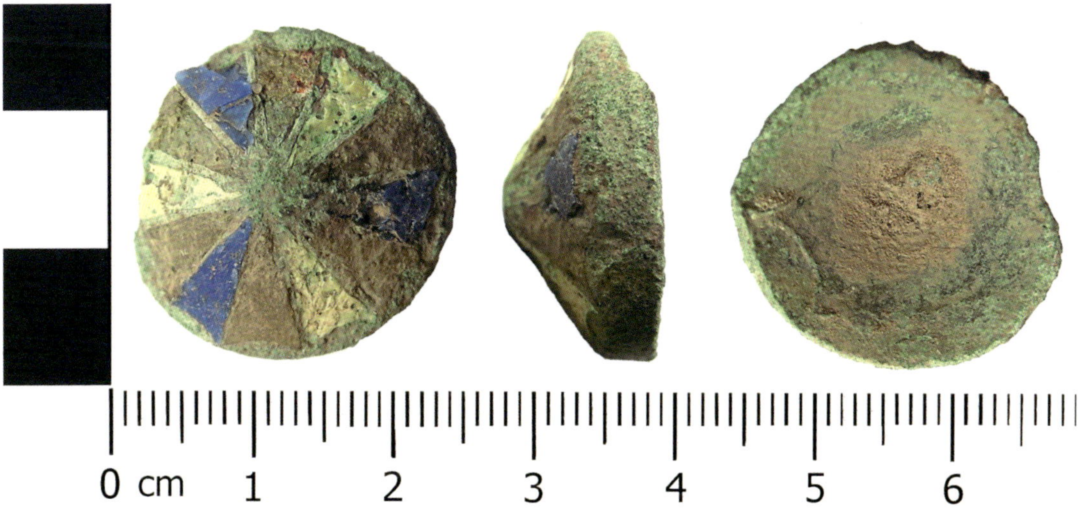

LANCUM-1AB886: Enamelled Roman disc brooch fragment from Longtown.

37. Roman gold necklace terminal from the Penrith area (LANCUM-4D5138)
AD 100–300
Length: 21 mm; Width: 19.8 mm; Weight: 1.69 g

Roman gold jewellery component, probably the terminal of a choker necklace. The surviving fragment consists of two identical decorative elements, one above the other, and formed of two layers of sheet gold, probably soldered together. Each consists of a plain backing plate and a hollow repoussé upper plate, in the form of two stylised and opposed birds. Each bird has a pellet eye, a ribbed beak and bodies composed of a series of parallel ribs to represent feathers. The decorative elements are well preserved, with the right-hand side of the lower element bent slightly upwards.

On the back of the decorative plates, there is an attachment hook consisting of a twist of wire, which has been hammered into a taper and rolled back on itself at its terminal. This is attached to a double loop of twisted wire, soldered to the upper backing plate. A similar double loop was passed through the loop formed by the upper wire, and soldered to the back of the lower decorative plate. This wire is slightly damaged, as the upper part of the loop has come adrift and is slightly bent. It seems likely that there was a further decorative element (or more), now missing.

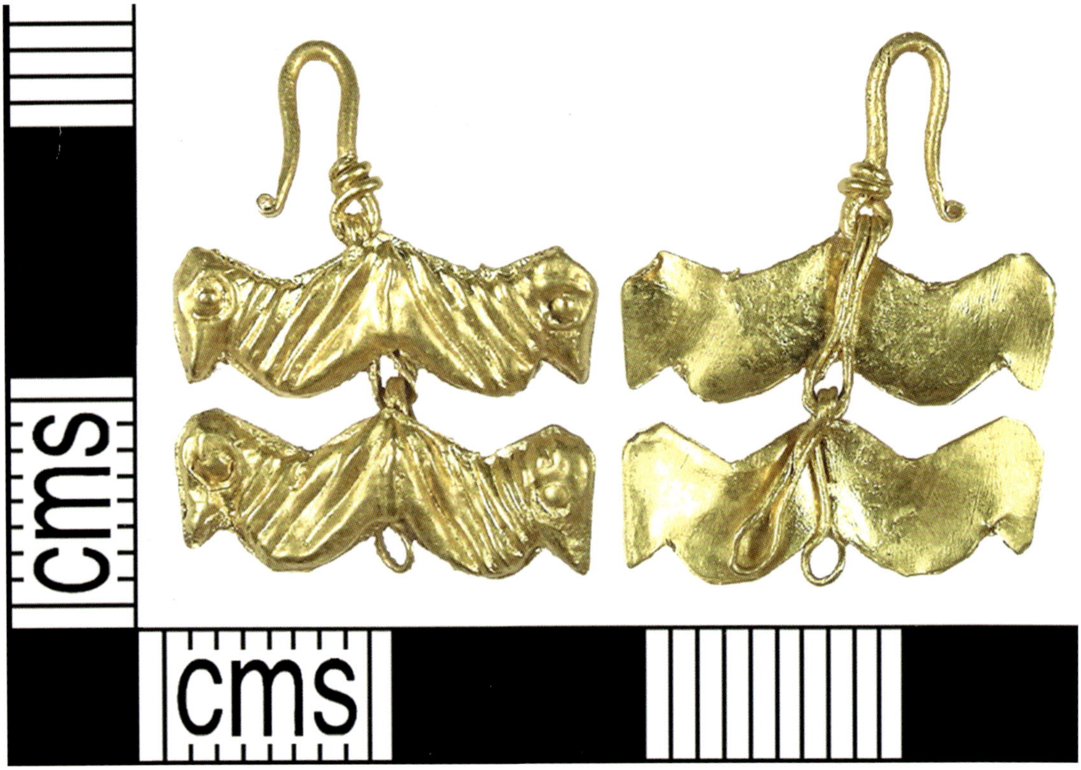

LANCUM-4D5138: Roman gold necklace terminal from the Penrith area.

28. A vessel from Beckfoot Roman cemetery (LANCUM-B497F1). Finds from same site (LANCUM-413CA5)
AD 100–300
Height: 85 mm; Thickness: 3.1 mm; Diameter: 61 mm

Small, complete accessory vessel (cup), dating from the second to third century. The cup survives intact and without a blemish. It is pear-shaped, with a small pedestal foot. It was made from local orange/pink-coloured clay, which was tempered with grit and small pieces of organic material. The outer surface is rough to the touch, as if it was 'sponged' to create a rougher, grippier surface on purpose. The inside surface is smooth. The vessel was an accessory vessel to a Roman cremation.

The small cup comes from Beckfoot, which is the site of a Roman cremation cemetery. Among many other complete vessels and sherds reported to the Portable Antiquities Scheme, there was also a complete cremation, made up of two vessels. While the urn was made from a north-western grey-ware vessel, a Dragendorff 27 imitation was used as the lid. The length is 220 mm, width 150 mm, diameter 110 mm, and the weight too heavy for scales.

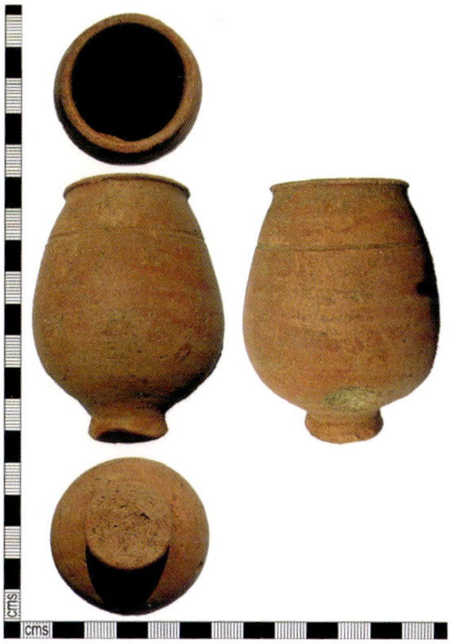

LANCUM-B497F1: A small coarseware cup (accessory vessel) from Beckfoot Roman cemetery.

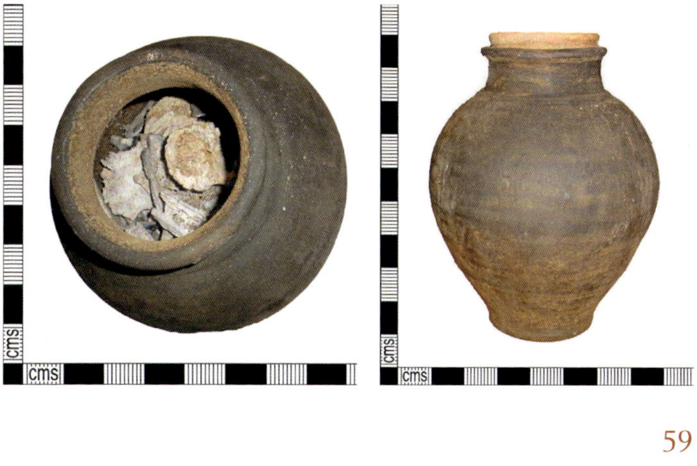

LANCUM-413CA5: A cremation vessel with Samian ware imitation for a lid.

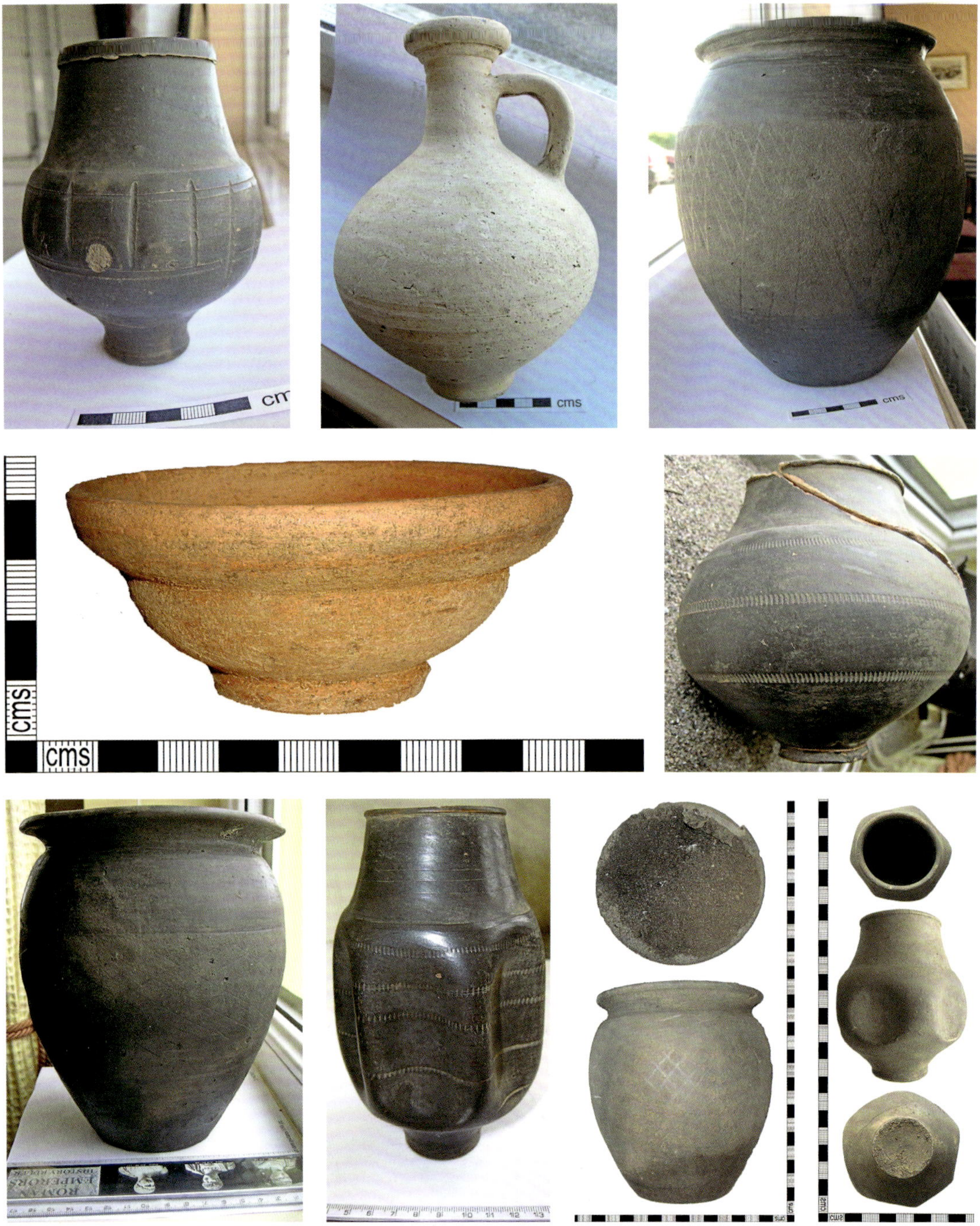

Several coarseware and fineware cups, urns, a flagon and an indented beaker were recorded from Beckfoot Roman cemetery. The first image in the second row is the small Dragendorff 27 imitation, which was used as the lid for Cremation vessel LANCUM-413CA5.

29. A Millefiori Pin fragment from the Crosby Ravensworth area (LANCUM-5ED187), and (LANCUM-E36A76)
AD 150–200
Thickness: 2 mm; Weight: 16.18 g; Diameter: 50 mm

An almost-complete cast copper-alloy millefiori mount, dating to the Roman period. The object is circular in plan and flat, with a small broken pin on the reverse. It is damaged and the outer rim is incomplete. Much of the enamel survives, and the millefiori squares can be seen the centre as well as the rings. On the obverse, the mount had three moulded rings, which held the enamel and millefiori pieces in at least three bands and the centre. The millefiori checkerboards were either nine squares or twenty-five squares, and were made up of white, black, blue and red glass. They were set in red enamelled centre and red and blue enamelled rings.

Millefiori is the name used to describe small polychrome patterns, made from thin rods of coloured glass. The patterns are made by arranging glass rods of various colours side by side, heating them just enough to fuse them together, and stretching the bundle of rods into a long, thin cane. Cold slices can be cut from the cane and used as part of enamelled designs.

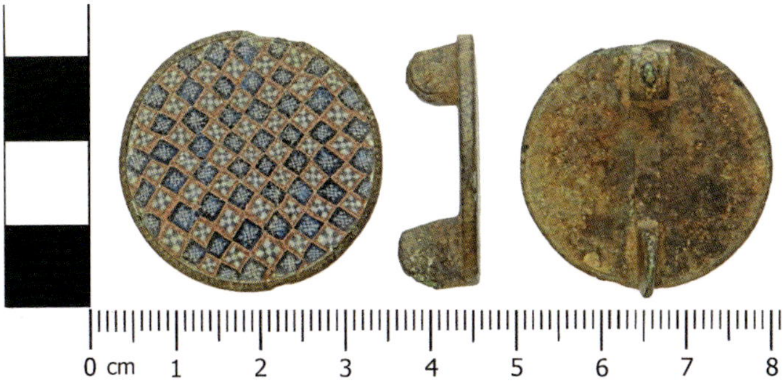

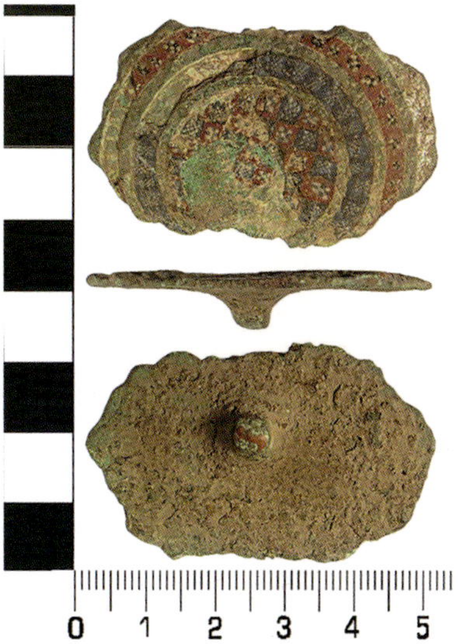

Above: LVPL-F1F6CC: Disc brooch with millefiori decoration.

Above right: LANCUM-5ED187: Millefiori mount or pin fragment from Crosby Ravensworth.

Below right: LANCUM-E36A76: Small pendant or mount decorated with millefiori.

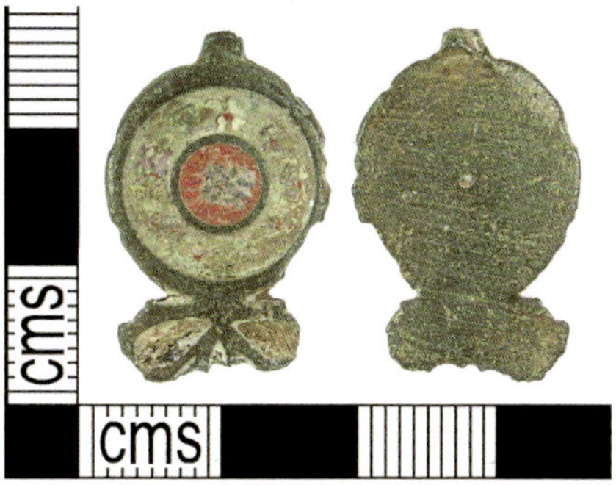

30. Button and loop fastener from the Cartmel Fell area (LANCUM-54B816)
AD 0–200
Length: 66 mm; Width: 38 mm; Thickness: 7 mm; Weight: 16.16 g

Unusually large cast copper-alloy button and loop fastener, dating from the late Iron Age/Roman period. The button and loop fastener consists of two fragments, which form a flat, circular disc. This has an openwork design that looks like three teardrop shapes in a row, which are formed by a curvilinear design. An arm is attached to the reverse of the disc, which is recessed and roughly triangular in shape; a cutaway triangular design on the reverse formed a bar on the end, where this part of the arm is hollow.

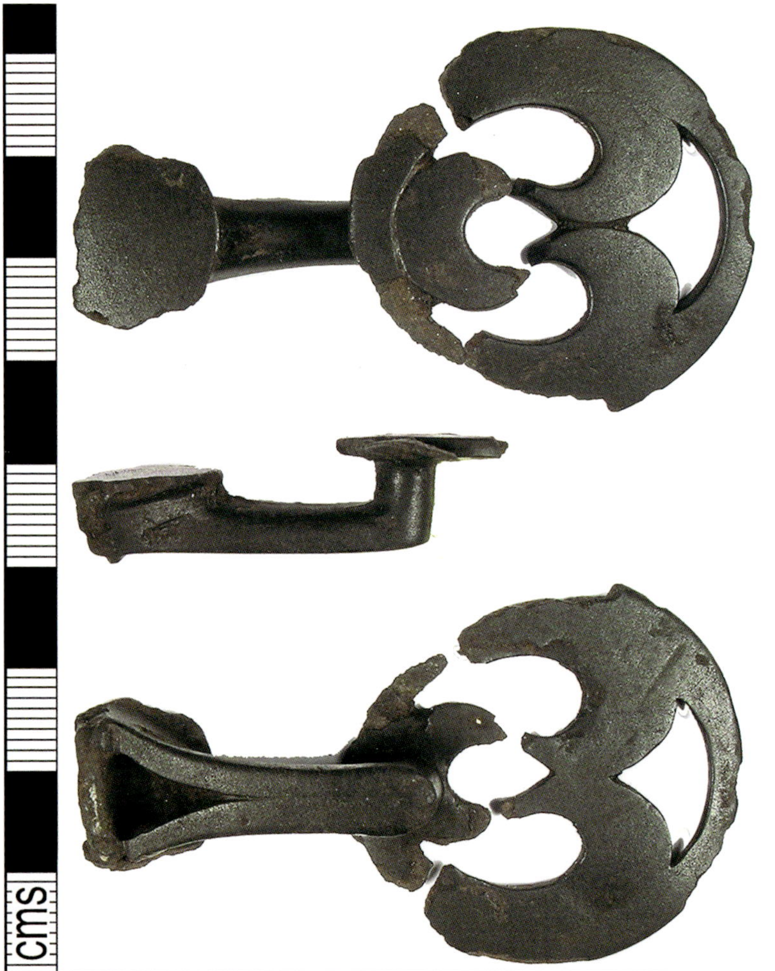

LANCUM-54B816: Button and loop fastener from Cartmel Fell.

Chapter 5
Early Medieval

Little is known about the so-called 'Dark Ages' in Cumbria – that is, the period between the ending of Roman rule in Britain (early fifth century AD) and the beginning of the medieval period (*c.* twelfth century AD), but we do know that, in these 700 years or so, massive social and cultural changes occurred. These changes were partly rooted in the use that the natives made of what the Romans had left them, and partly in what the new settlers and invaders from Scandinavia brought with them.

When the Roman Empire abandoned Britain in the fifth century AD, there was no immediate or sudden breakdown of control. In Cumbria, archaeological evidence strongly suggests that the Romanised way of life continued well into the fifth century. However, it seems that, once Rome's central rule had ended, the power over land and resources fell to a number of rulers with smaller territories and ever-changing boundaries. In sixth-century Cumbria, one of these smaller kingdoms developed into what was called 'Rheged'; another century later, Cumbria may have possibly been incorporated – through marriage, heritage or military alliance – into the kingdom of Northumbria, which was part of the heptarchy of Anglo-Saxon kingdoms.

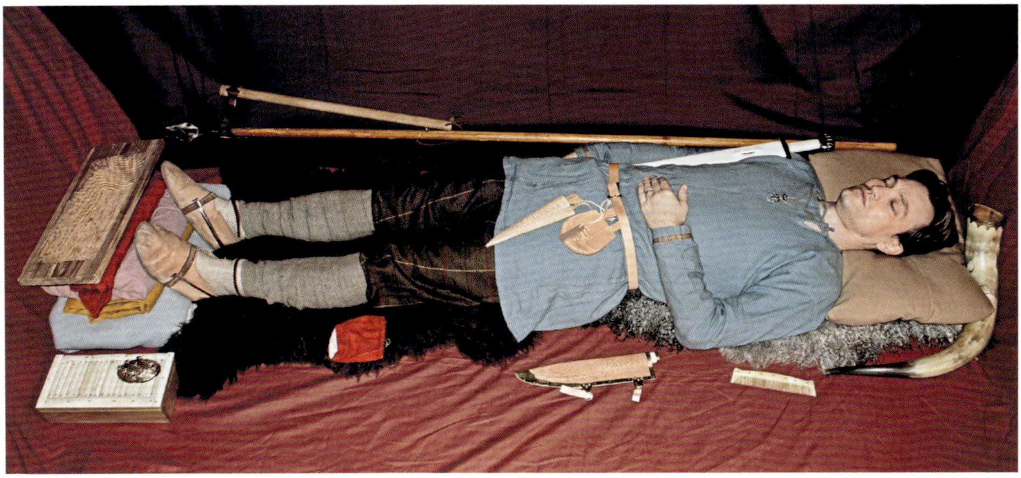

A modern reconstruction of the burial in Grave 5 from Cumwhitton Viking cemetery. (Oxford Archaeology Ltd)

From the end of the eighth century, the Vikings enter Britain, first as raiders, then as settlers: they are called 'Northmen' for their origin or 'Vikings' for what was possibly their profession. 'Viking' probably meant both 'maritime warrior' and 'military maritime expansion or exploration'. These Northmen were formidable shipbuilders and navigators and fearless raiders and warriors. In their society, rulers relied on the loyalty of their followers, many of whom will have received their share of the loot or land in return.

There is no sufficient archaeological evidence anywhere in the north-west to indicate much Viking settlement before the early tenth century, and there is little artefactual evidence for 'Viking everyday life' recorded on the PAS database. In fact, most of the Cumbrian early-medieval material consists of Treasure finds – which, coincidentally, come from the same areas where place names suggest early-medieval settlement: these are west and south-west Cumbria (the Furness Hoard, no. 36, and the mount from Arnside, no. 41), the Eden Valley (Cumwhitton, no. 37) and the area east of Carlisle, around Brampton and Irthington (nos 33 and 35).

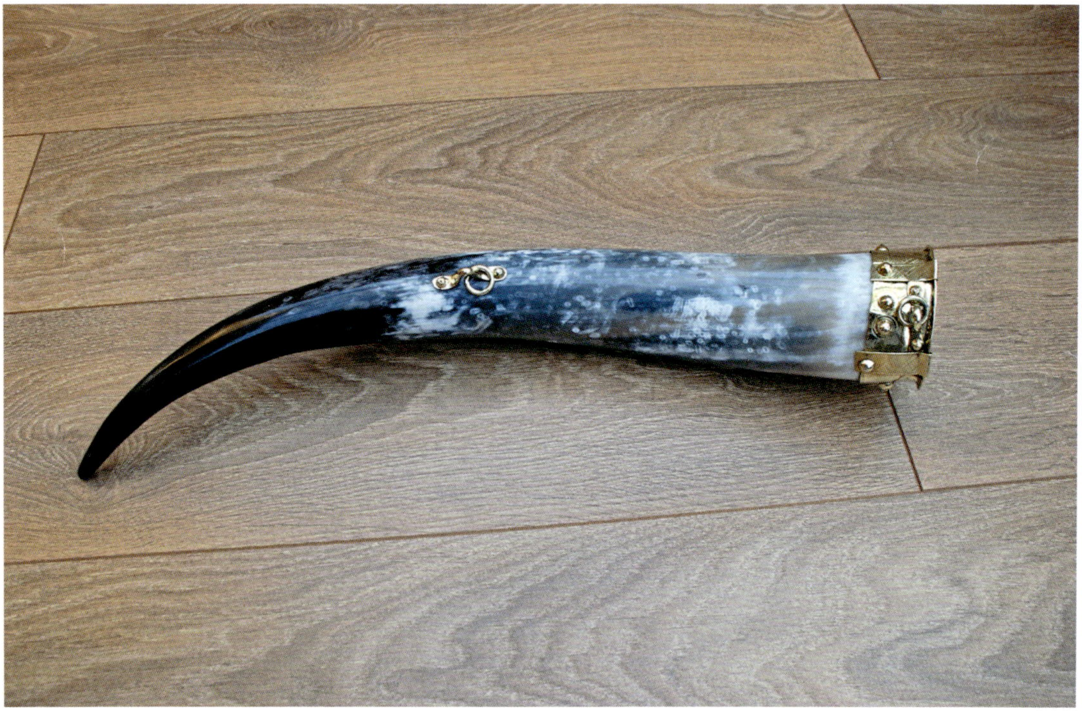

Replica of the drinking horn found in Grave 2, Cumwhitton Viking cemetery. (Copyright Adam Parsons)

31. Gold tremissis from Burton in Kendal (LANCUM-3E51D8)
AD 620–640.
Diameter: 13 mm; Weight: 1.27 g.

This is the only early medieval Merovingian gold tremissis of Drondrijp type from Cumbria. It was probably minted in Austrasia (north-eastern section of the Merovingian kingdom in the seventh/eight centuries) or Frisia (modern Low Countries) and dating *c.* 620–40.

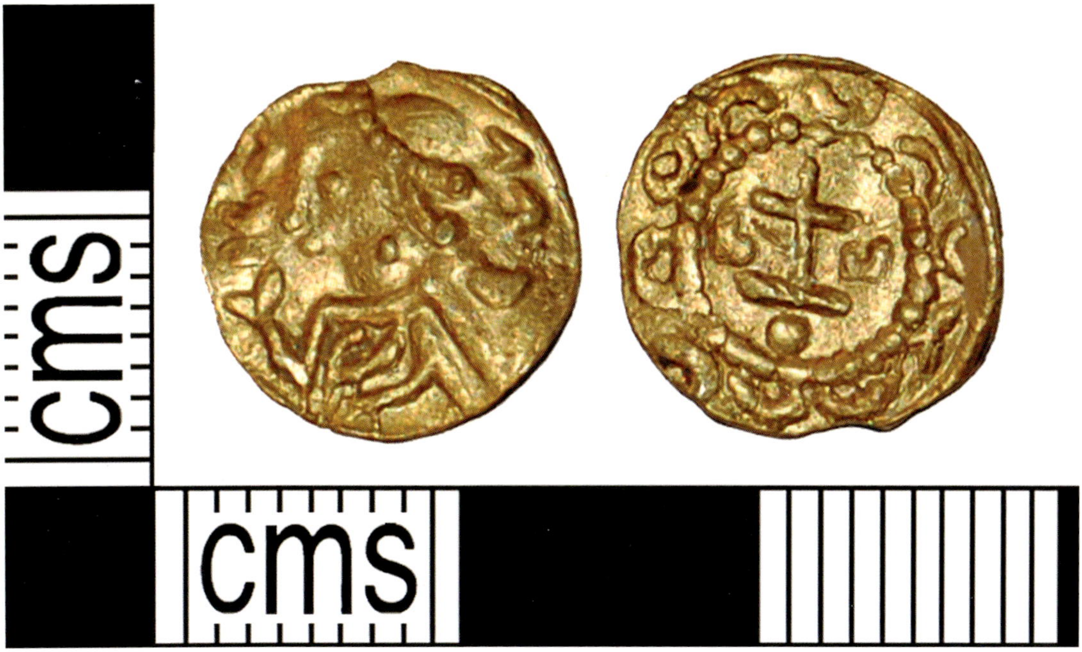

LANCUM-3E51D8: Gold tremissis from Burton in Kendal.

32. Aspatria Type strap end from Cockermouth (LANCUM-E1BD74)
AD 900–1100
Length: 26 mm; Width: 21 mm; Thickness: 2.5 mm

An incomplete cast copper-alloy strap end, dating from the early medieval period and the tenth to eleventh century AD. This class of strap ends are named after the Viking grave assemblage from Aspatria (Cumbria). The surface of the strap end from Cockermouth retains some tinning in the crevices of the decoration. The complete strap end was tongue shaped, with a split terminal at the flat end, which is missing here. It would probably have had two rivet holes in the upper part of both front and back plate. The upper surface of the strap end is decorated with a tongue shaped panel, denoted by an incised border within, which is a geometric design featuring 'X' shapes, joined by a central vertical line. Only one and the upper half of another X remain. The arms of the 'X's are bent and decorated with a small number of ring-and-dot punches. The reverse is flat and undecorated.

There is a number of similar strap ends, most of which come from either the East Riding of Yorkshire or Cumbria: YORYM-AF4D02 (Yapham, East Riding of Yorkshire), LANCUM-789A57 (Maulds Meaburn, Cumbria), YORYM-FDF9D2 (Market Weighton, East Riding of Yorkshire) and another one was discovered in Grave 2 at Cumwhitton, Cumbria.

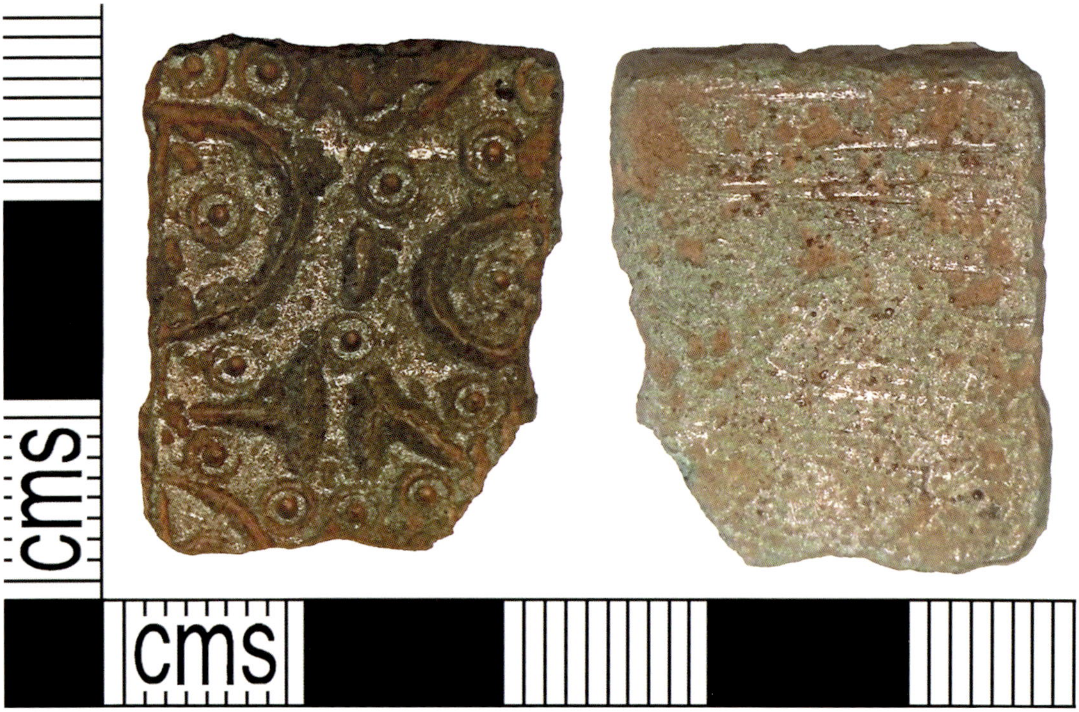

LANCUM-E1BD74: Aspatria Type strap end from Cockermouth.

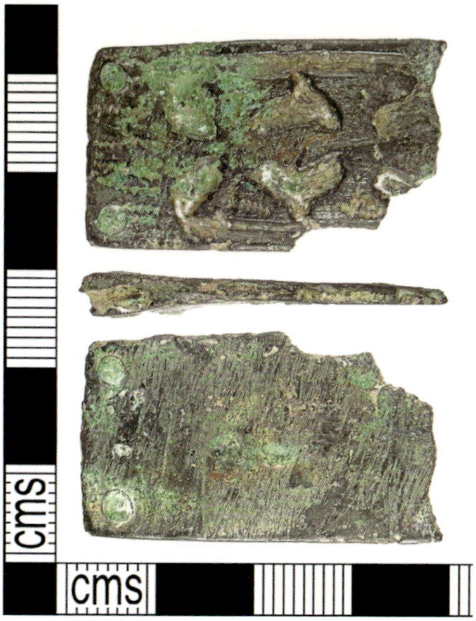

LANCUM-789A57: Aspatria type strap end from Maulds Meaburn, Cumbria.

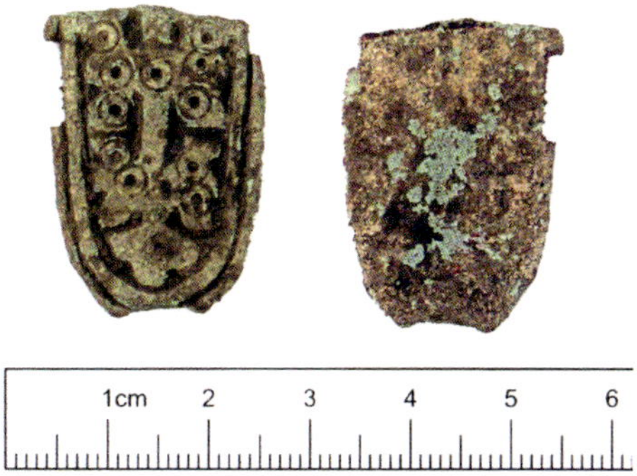

YORYM-AF4DO2: Aspatria type strap end from Yapham, East Riding of Yorkshire.

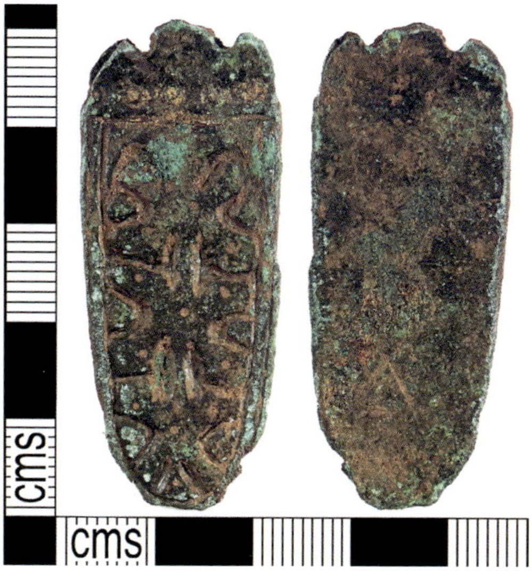

YORYM-FDF9D2: Aspatria type strap end from Market Weighton, East Riding of Yorkshire.

33. Viking pomander pendant from the Irthington area (LANCUM-FD0AD2)

AD 1000–1050
Length: 34.99 mm; Height: 13.3 mm; Width: 19.9 mm; Weight: 15.29 g

Viking silver pendant. The pendant is tear-shaped, hollow, and convex at the front, with an integral loop at the top for suspension. The front is decorated, with an incised, diagonal, cruciform design, formed by four tear-shapes with their broad ends pointing towards the centre, which is pierced by a hole within a circle. There are four other holes at the cardinal points, and the design is enclosed by two grooves, the upper one curving in arcs round the outer holes. A further groove round the edge of the base is joined to the lower groove at each side by two short, vertical lines. The back is flat, with a raised circle in the centre that is pierced by an irregular hole. Beneath the loop at the front is a raised V-shape.

The perforations on the front suggest that the pendant may have been filled with an aromatic substance for use as a sort of pomander; however, analyses at the British Museum of the associated soil sample from inside the pendant have not been able to establish any evidence for plant material or resin.

Compare this with another three-dimensional silver object, this time of late eight- or ninth-century date: CAM-4DB246 (from Broxted, Essex). Also pictured are two other English objects, decorated with a cross made by removing four drop shapes from a circle are BERK-8E4641 (from Boxford, West Berkshire), a die stamp thought to be of late seventh-century date; and LIN-1C1D22 (from Little Carlton, Lincolnshire), a possible pin head thought to be of eighth-century date.

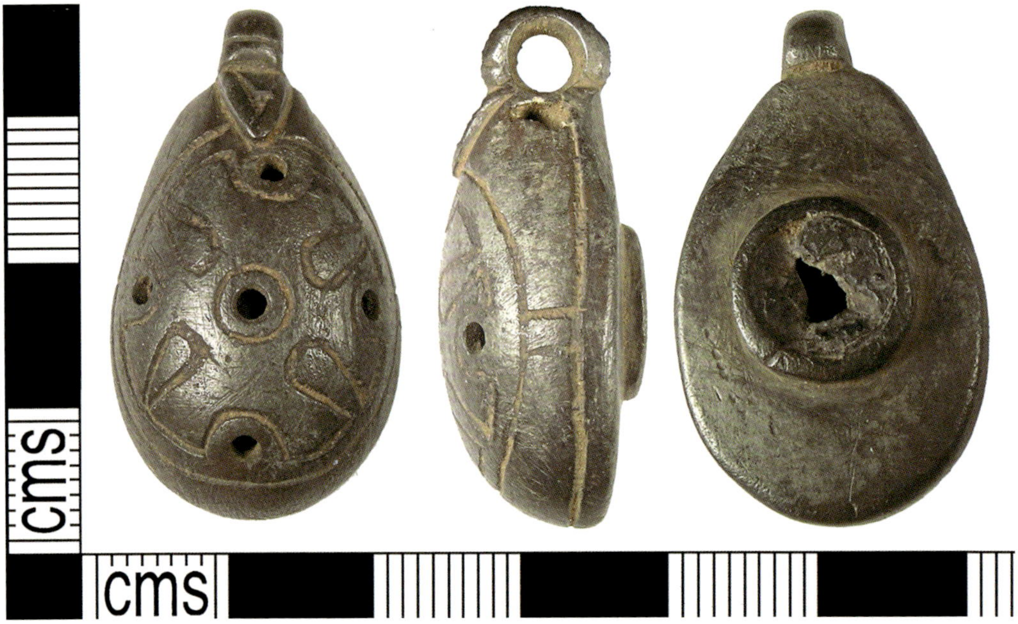

LANCUM-FD0AD2: Viking pomander pendant from the Irthington area.

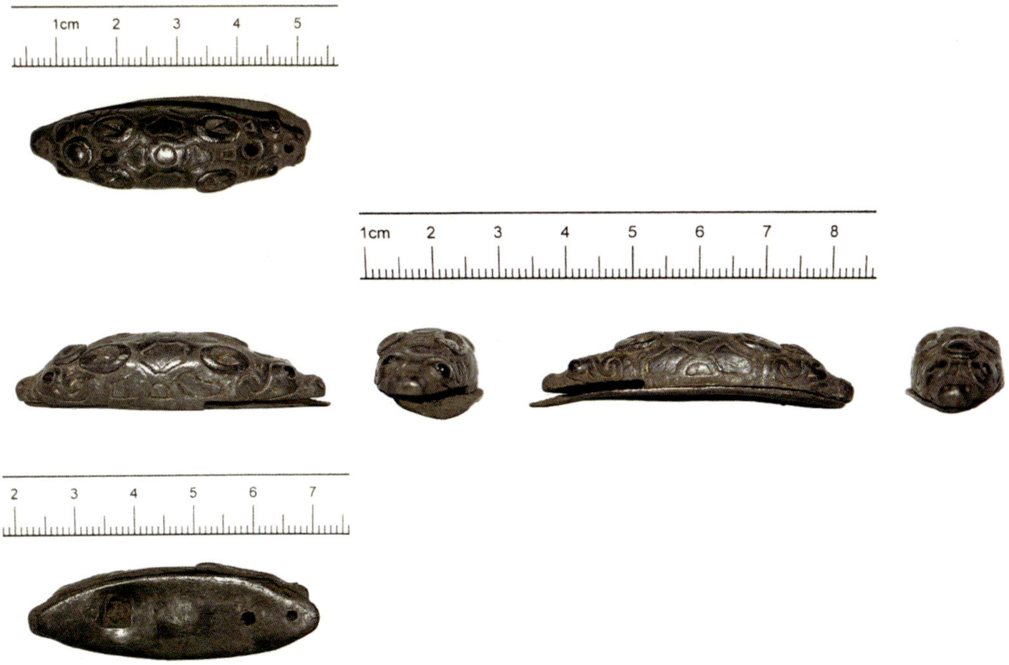

CAM-4DB246: Unidentified early medieval silver object.

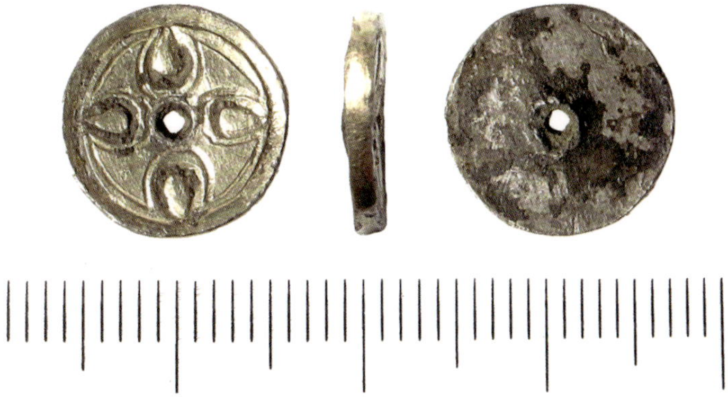

LIN-1C1D22:
Eighth-century pin head.

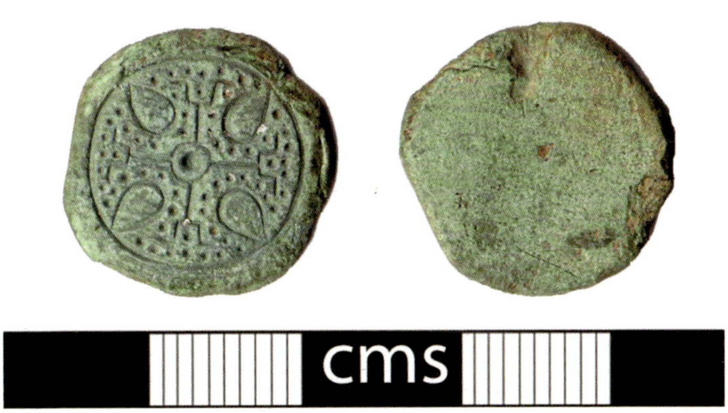

BERK-8E4641: Early medieval die stamp.

34. Gold ring from Sedbergh (LANCUM-ED5E96)

AD 900–1100

Length: 25.09 mm; Width: 23.21 mm; Thickness: 1.69 mm; Weight: 13.7 g

A Viking gold ring, consisting of a double-banded hoop made from a slightly concavo-convex strip, with the ends drawn into wires at the back of the hoop, which are then tightly wound round a constricted section of the strip (fig. 34). The bands are very slightly apart at the front and sides. They are both incised with a median groove decorated above and below with two rows of small, punched, apex-to-apex triangles, creating slightly raised lozenge shapes. The spacing of the punches is irregular in places.

The form of the ring is closely comparable with two Viking examples, also of gold, in the collection of the British Museum, with only two coils each from Saddleworth Moor (Greater Manchester) and Ireland, although they are made of rods rather than a strip. The form is further paralleled by a distinctive type of coiled silver arm ring, made in Ireland in the late ninth/early tenth centuries and developed from a simpler Viking type. A further example of this type from Maunby in North Yorkshire was recently reported as treasure (NCL-FEC824).

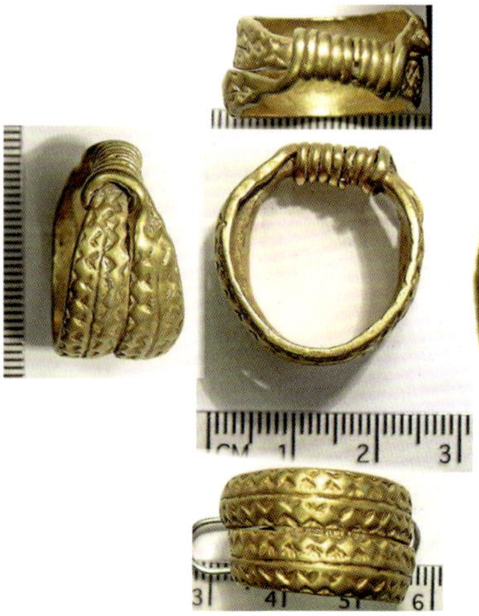

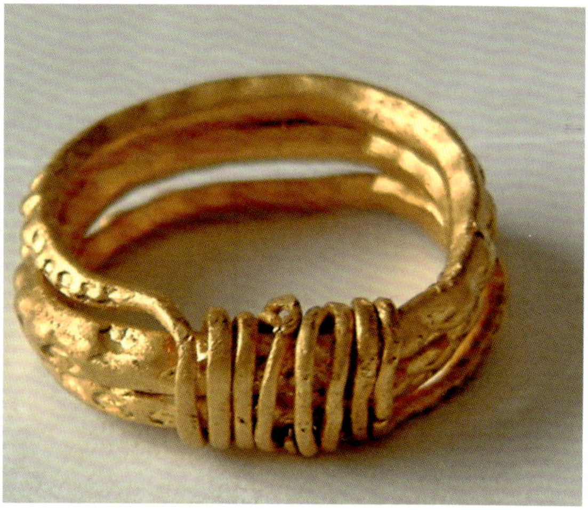

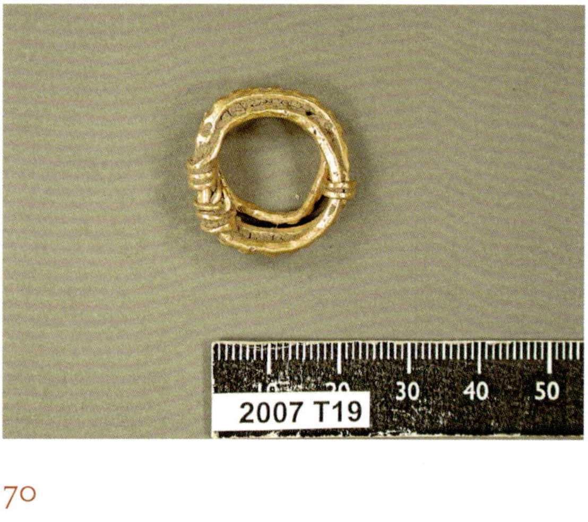

Above left: LANCUM-ED5E96: Gold ring from Sedbergh.

Above right: NCL-FEC824: Gold ring from Maunby, North Yorkshire (close up).

Left: NCL-FEC824: Gold ring from Maunby, North Yorkshire.

35. Thor's hammer from the Longtown area (LANCUM-ED9222)

AD 850–1000

Length: 47.13 mm; Width: 21.16 mm; Thickness: 3.77 mm; Weight: 12.19 g

The pendant is cast in the form of a plain, flat, double-headed hammer, with a concave-sided central projection on top and a long, slightly concave-sided shaft of rectangular section. The end of the shaft is broken across a hole for suspension, and the surface abrasions are both original and a typical feature of Viking-period silver objects.

The object belongs to a series of Viking-period amuletic pendants, thought to represent Mjøllnir, the hammer of the mighty Norse god Thor. They are found widely distributed in areas of Viking settlement, from England (in the Danelaw and the northwest), Iceland and Normandy to Scandinavia and Russia. They occur in male and female graves, hoards and settlement sites. At least fifty silver examples are known.

About a dozen English examples are known, mostly of silver. Some of them may have been made in the Danelaw, including two examples from Lincolnshire (from Torksey and Spilsby). The English ones are mostly plain, or only simply decorated, e.g., the silver example from the Cuerdale hoard, Lancs. This dates to the late ninth century or beginning of the tenth century, and has a long shaft, like the Longtown find, although it ends in a loop rather than a hole for suspension.

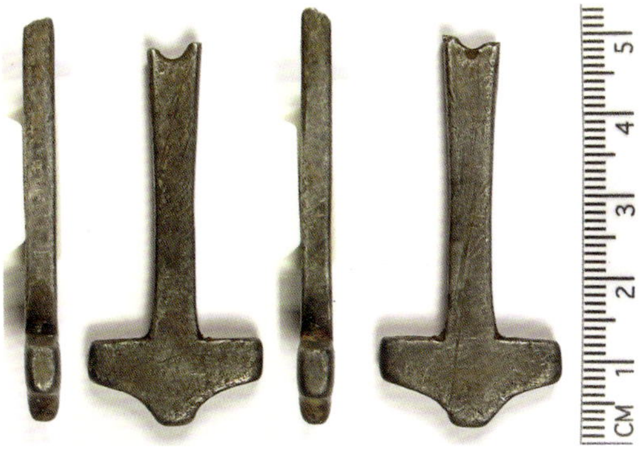

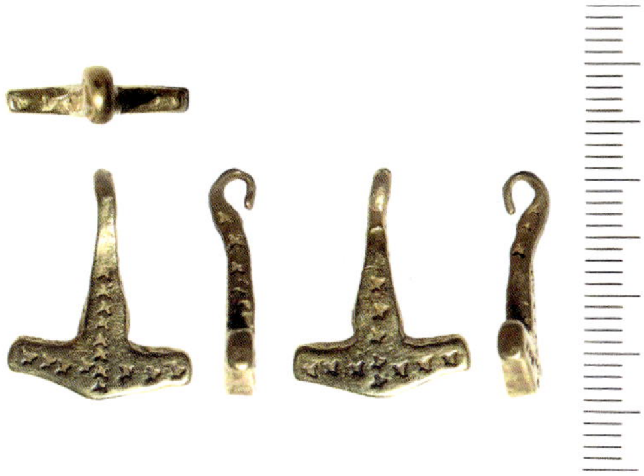

Above left: LANCUM-ED9222: Thor's hammer from the Longtown area.

Above right: LIN-D3E540: Thor's hammer from the Spilsby area (Lincolnshire).

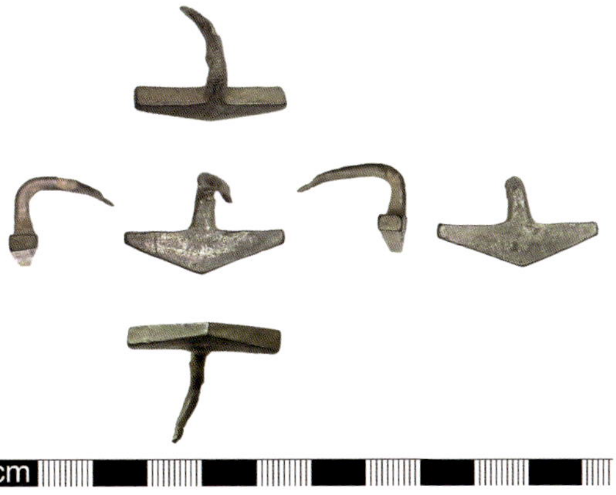

Right: DENO-BD0oC3: Thor's hammer from the Torksey area (Lincolnshire).

36 Furness hoard (LANCUM 80A304)

AD 950–1000

A Viking-age hoard, consisting of seventy-nine coins (twenty-two of which are fragments) and thirteen silver-ingot fragments. The non-numismatic items in the hoard are all of diagnostically Viking manufacture and/or show typically Viking secondary treatment, such as pieces hacked for use of bullion or showing test marks to establish the quality of the silver. Some of these pieces are generically Viking, while others have particular parallels in Viking finds from northern England, Scotland and around the Irish Sea. The coins come from a mixture of sources: they are predominantly Anglo-Saxon pennies, with a smaller number of Anglo-Viking pennies, and two Islamic dirhams. This mixture of coin types is again typically Viking, as is the combination of coinage and non-numismatic silver in a single hoard, and there is no reason to doubt that all of the objects reported derive from a single hoard.

A number of comparable Viking hoards have been recorded from tenth-century England, although typically they date from the first three decades of the century, around or before the unification of England under Athelstan in AD 927. Although a few of the coins (and perhaps some of the non-numismatic objects) date from the early tenth century, both the Anglo-Saxon and Anglo-Viking coins show a concentration in the 940s and 950s, reflecting in part the resurgence of Viking power in northern England at this time, culminating in the death of Eirik Haraldsson (normally identified with Eirik Bloodaxe of Norway) in 954. However, the presence of a significant number of coins from the end of the reign of Eadred (946–55), and from the reign of Eadwig (955–59), combined with the absence of any coins of his younger brother Eadgar (957/959–975), suggests a deposition date of *c.* 955–57, after the Viking resurgence had been suppressed. In particular, the hoard shows a continued influx of coins minted in York and/or the East Midlands after the death of Eirik in 954. This is an unusually late date for a Viking hoard from northern England, but western Cumbria almost certainly still lay beyond the borders of the emerging kingdom of England at this time. The hoard shows greater affinities with Viking hoards of the same period from Scotland, Ireland and the Isle of Man, reflecting the proximity of the Furness area to the economic area of the Irish Sea, as well as the strong evidence for Viking settlement across the North West in the form of place names, sculpture and other hoards.

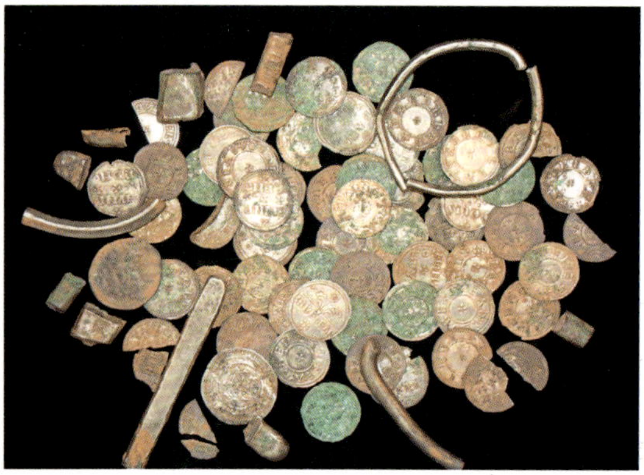

LANCUM-80A304: The Furness hoard. (Dock Museum, Barrow-in-Furness)

Penny of Anlaf Guthfrithsson dating from *c.* AD 939–941, minted at York by Aethelferth.

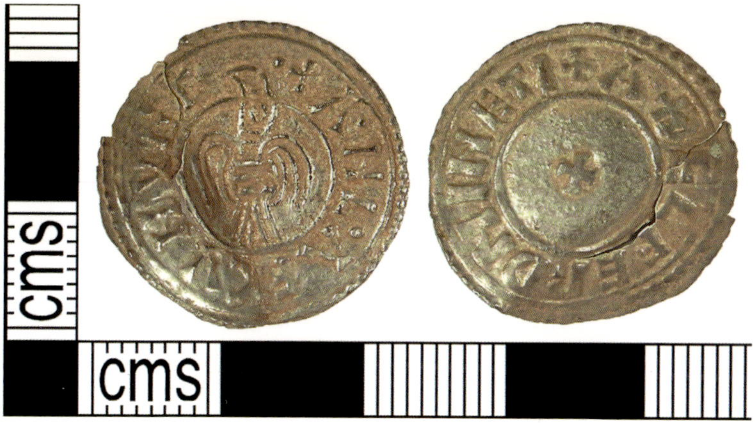

Penny of Archbishop Plegmund dating from *c.* AD 899–924, minted at Canterbury by Ethelstan.

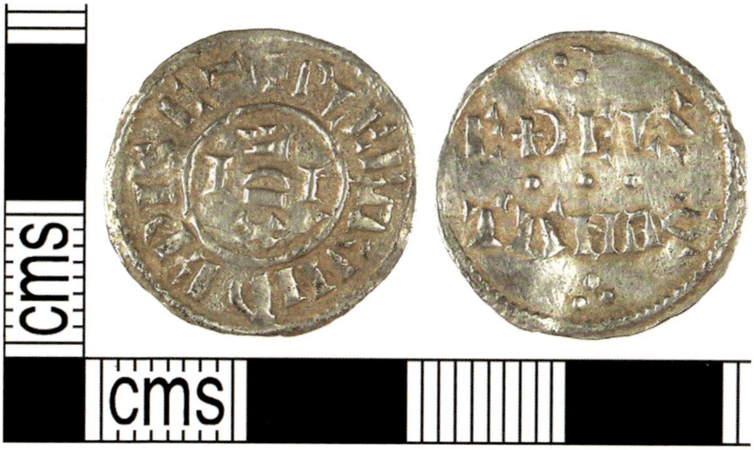

Penny of Aethelstan dating from *c.* AD 9245–939, minted at Chester by Sigeferth.

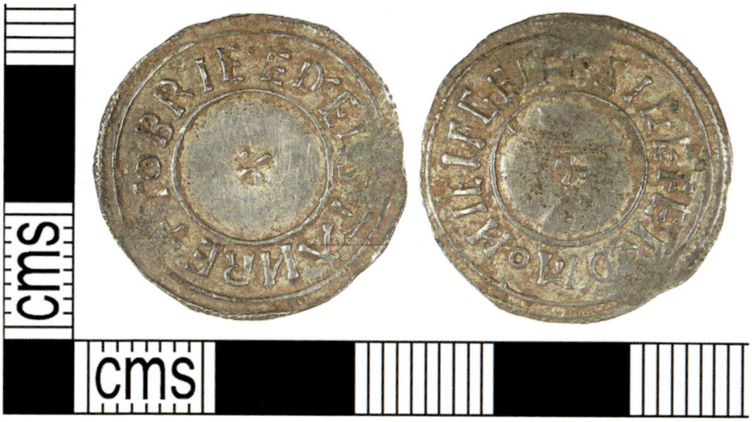

37. Viking graves from Cumwhitton: ring (LANCUM-972281) and brooch (LON-F2F201)

AD 900–925

In 2004, a Cumbrian metal-detectorist discovered a large openwork oval brooch while out metal-detecting near Cumwhitton in the Eden Valley. The then-county archaeologist for Lancashire, Ben Edwards, identified the brooch as a rare Viking oval brooch of the eighth or ninth century, and noted that these are normally found in pairs in burial contexts, not as random depositions or losses. The detectorist went back to the find site and did indeed find the other brooch, too. This was a discovery of national importance, and Oxford Archaeology North, funded by English Heritage, first evaluated and then excavated the site. It turned out to be a small cemetery of six graves, dating from the early tenth century and thus contemporary with the deposition of the Cuerdale and Silverdale hoards in Lancashire.

The six burials were ostentatious and a wide range of artefacts survived, such as swords, spurs, knives, spearheads, finger rings, amber and glass beads, ring pins and the two oval brooches.

Even though there was next-to-no survival of organic remains such as bones and wood, the excavations revealed the presence of a box that was placed at the feet of one of the deceased, shears and a possible needle case, as well as a linen-smoother.

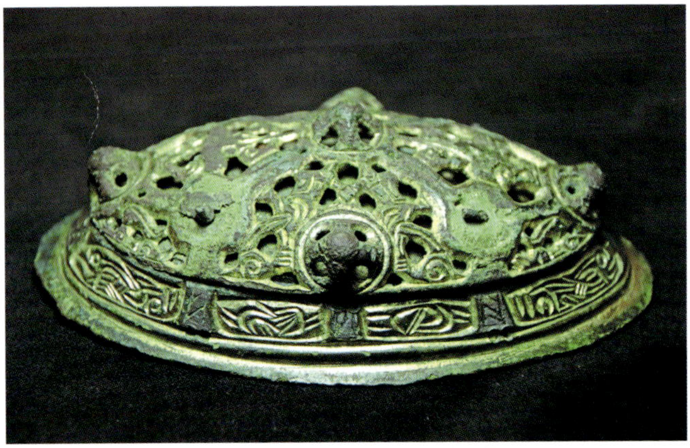

Close-up of one of the oval brooches from Grave 1, after conservation. (Oxford Archaeology Ltd)

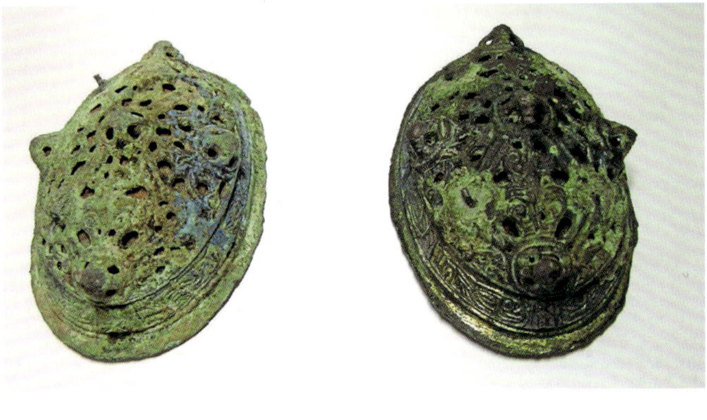

LON-F2F201: The two oval brooches from Grave 1, Cumwhitton Viking cemetery.

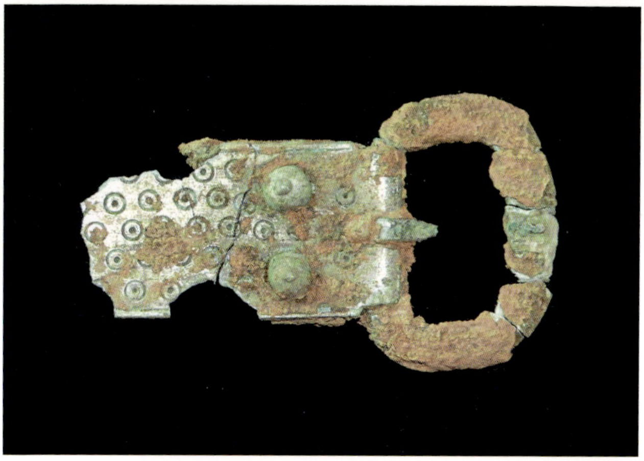

Belt buckle found in Grave 2. (Oxford Archaeology Ltd)

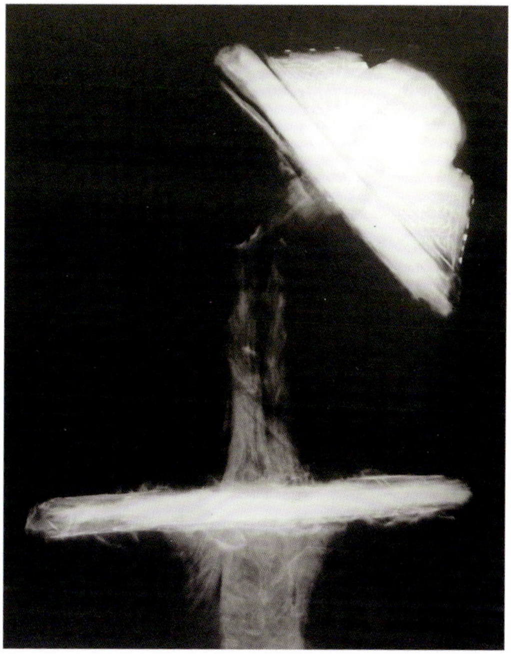

X-ray revealing the intricate decoration of the pommel and guard on the sword from Grave 3. (Oxford Archaeology Ltd)

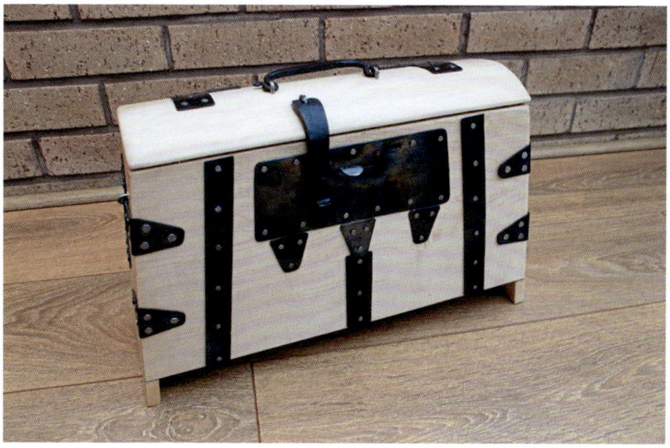

Exact replica of the wooden box found in Grave 5. (Adam Parsons)

38. Lead weight with bronze inset from the Kirkoswald area (LANCUM-1943D1)
AD 800–1000
Length: 21 mm; Width: 20 mm; Thickness: 13 mm; Weight: 41.79 g

Viking cast lead-alloy trade weight, dating from the early medieval period: the ninth or tenth century. The weight comprises a cut fragment of ornamental cast copper-alloy metalwork (possibly gilt), set into a lead base. The item appears complete. It is of flat cubic shape, with the ornamental copper-alloy inset, covering all of the upper surface. There is a circular piece of copper alloy sticking out of the lower surface, but this may have been the spike of the copper-alloy mount, which was hammered flat against the surface of the square lead weight. The decoration of the copper-alloy piece is simple: a small square surrounded by four L-shapes with arms of equal length. The interior of the smaller geometrical shapes is scratched/roughened up, possibly to receive and hold enamel. A very similar lead weight from Cardiff (NMGW-07268F) depicts the same ornament, although a different arrangement of it.

In the Viking period weights are believed to have been used for weighing precious metals while trading. Corrosion and some peripheral loss, together with differing systems of weighing, now make it difficult to suggest an original unit weight. There are several examples from Cumbria: two are from the Furness area and another, slightly more unusual one was recorded from Crosby Ravensworth (LANCUM-683C84).

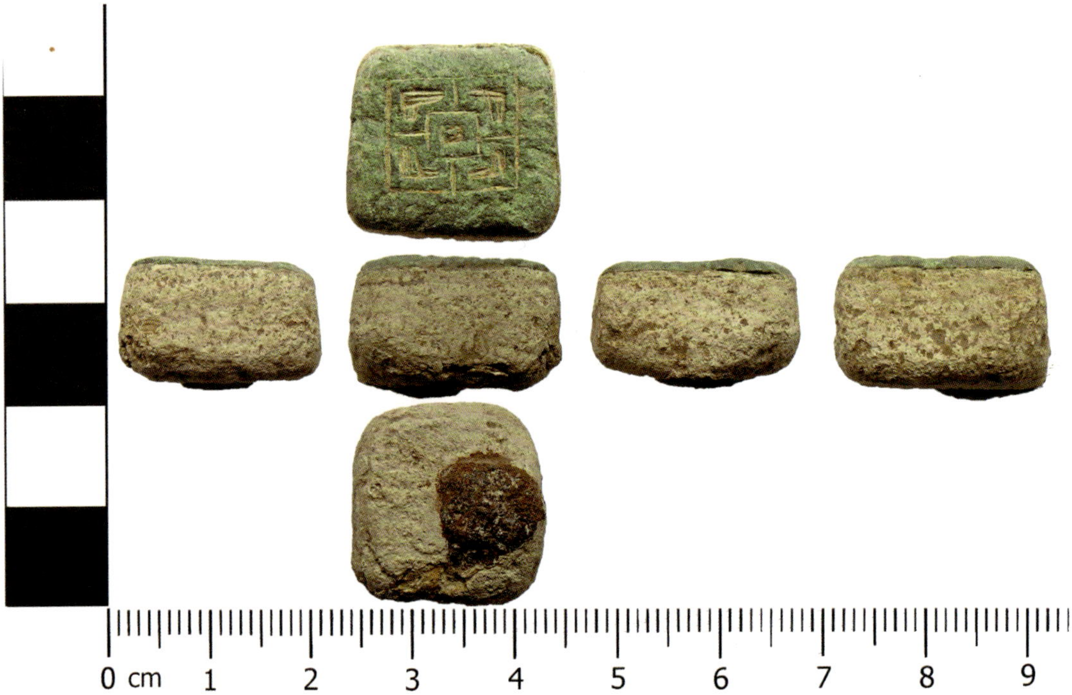

LANCUM-1943D1: Early medieval lead weight with gilt copper-alloy inset from the Kirkoswald area.

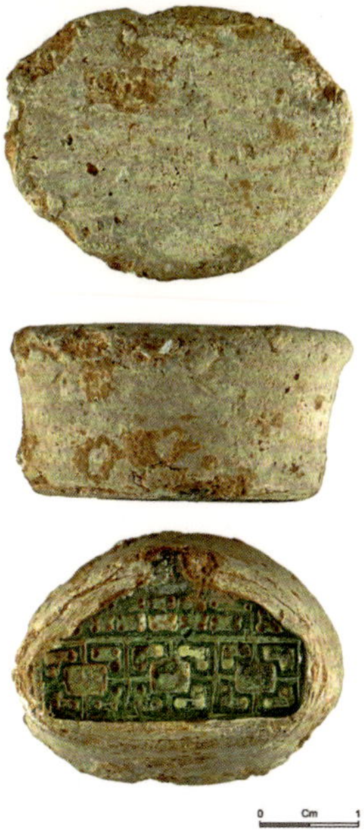

NMGW-07268F: Lead weight from Wenvoe, Glamorgan.

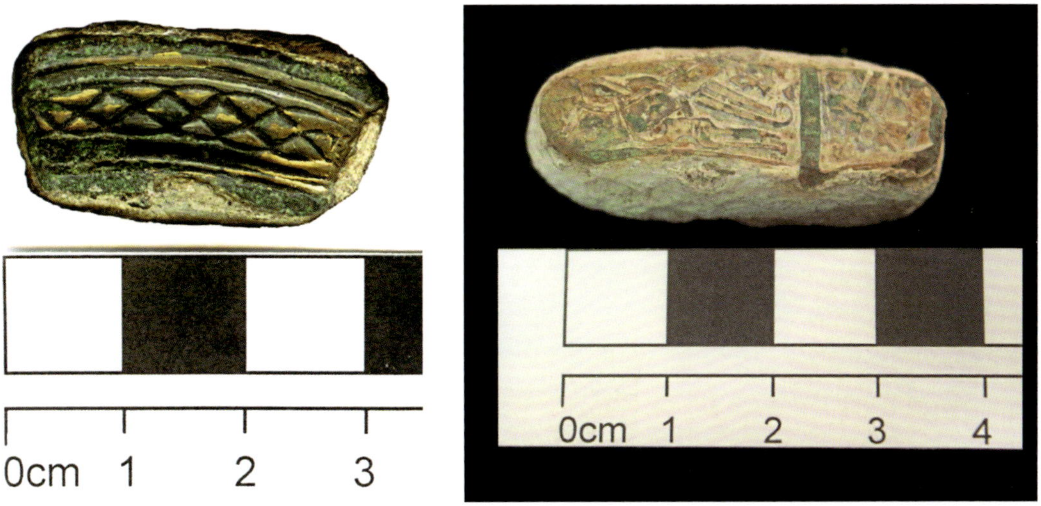

Two early medieval lead weights with gilt copper-alloy insets from the Furness area.

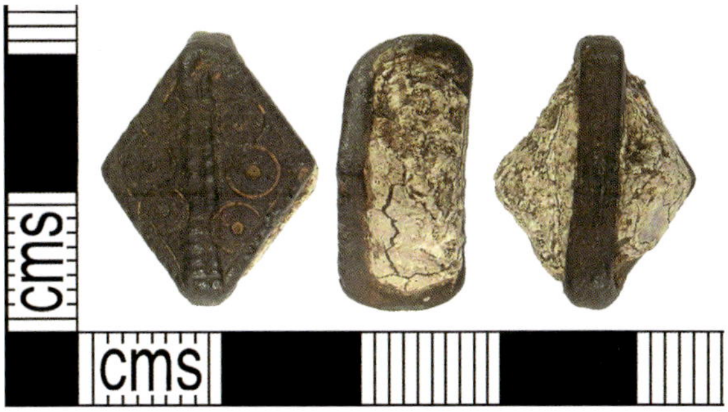

LANCUM-683C84: Early medieval lead weight encased in copper-alloy with stamped ring-and-dot motif.

39. Early medieval pin from Arnside (LVPL2205)
AD 700–800
Length: 32 mm; Width: 19.6 mm

Parabolic cast bronze plate, with cast ornament on one face, riveted to a second, smaller cast bronze plate of darker metal. The main plate originally ended with a rectangular projection, which is now replaced by another piece. It is pierced twice for rivets at the apex and has another neat hole by the edge, midway down one side; this hole has a neat internal edge, as if countersunk from the back. The plate carries cast ornament in chip-carved style, with a broad border of oblique lines around a subtriangular panel of neat looped interlace. This is a composite piece, manufactured in antiquity, and appears to be a decorative plate reused as an improvised head for a dress pin or stylus. The original projecting strip suggests that it was originally a box fitting.

Early medieval metalwork or recycled earlier metalwork, such as this pin or the aforementioned weights, are rare in Cumbria. A parallel for the find from Lorton, however, is this mount from Arnside, dating from the eighth or ninth century AD (LANCUM-B494A4). The perforated disc is broken and damaged around the outer edges. Originally, it was crescentic, with possibly a central inset stone (or similar). While the obverse is decorated, the reverse is plain. The surfaces are pitted but, otherwise, the object is in good condition. The decoration on the obverse consists of moulded concentric circles, with ribbed, triangular and herringbone/rope pattern mouldings in turn. The obverse shows remains of gilding in the crevices of the mouldings.

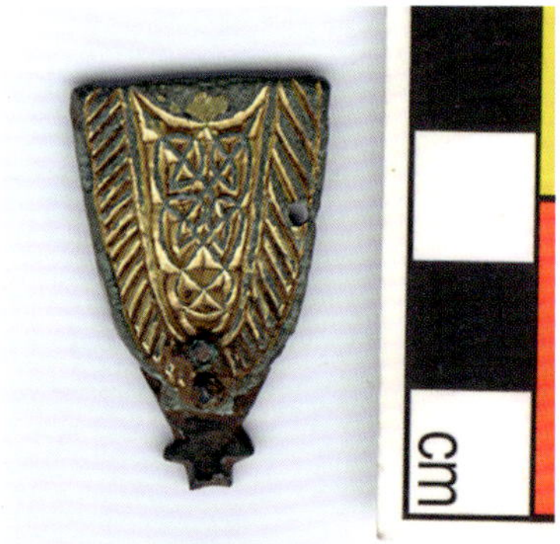

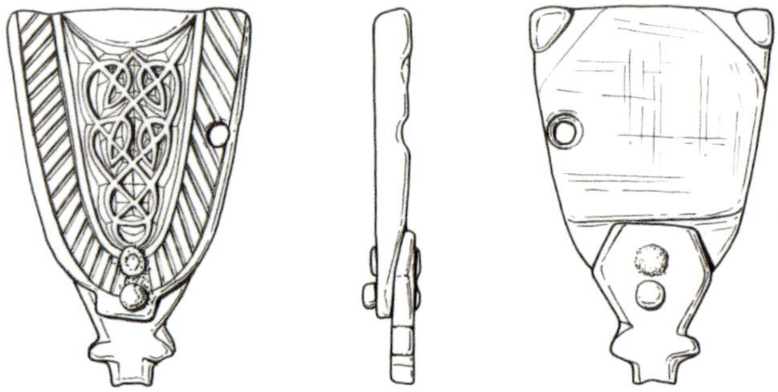

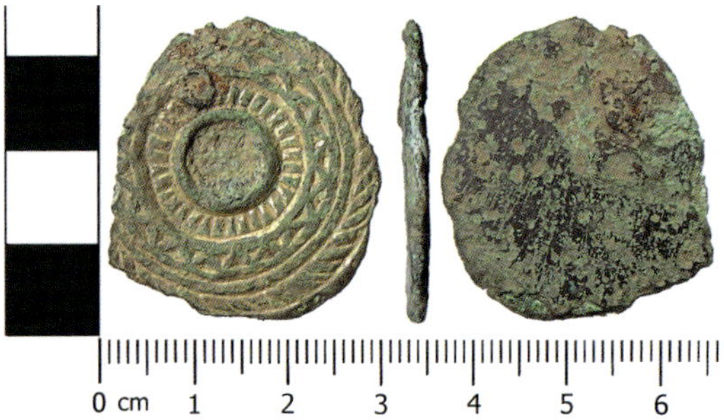

Above left: LVPL2205: Early medieval pin from Arnside.

Above right: LVPL2205: Early medieval pin from Arnside (drawing).

Left: LANCUM-B494A3: Fragment of an early medieval pin from Lorton, Cumbria.

40. Drinking horn terminal from Burton in Kendal: LANCUM-E89D32
AD 900–1050
Length: 50 mm; Width: 15 mm; Thickness: 1.5 mm; Weight: 30.05 g; Diameter: 15 mm

Silver drinking horn terminal dating from the early medieval period, the tenth to the eleventh century AD. The terminal is in the form of a slightly tapered socket, terminating in a cast, three-dimensional animal head, probably representing a lion with a very worn, rounded snout. At the triple-scalloped, open end of the socket, the uppermost of three projections survives, modelled in the form of a small animal head with drilled eyes and arc-punched ears. On either side of and underneath the neck of the socket are three further rivet holes. In the one on the left, a silver rivet survives, suggesting that there may have been material from the original horn present within the terminal, which has been scraped out recently, leaving bright scratches on the metal.

The zoomorphic form of the terminal is comparable in broad terms with silver terminal of the mid-to late Anglo-Saxon period from Barrowby, Lincolnshire (LIN-DA87D8).

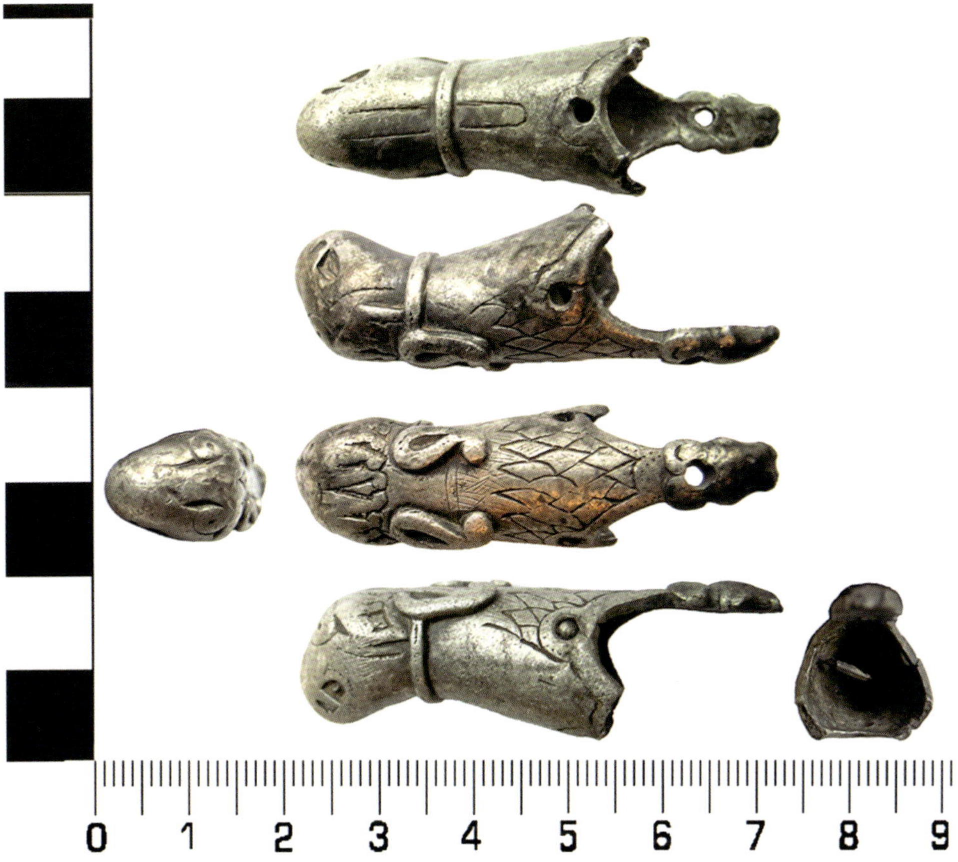

LANCUM-E89D32: Drinking horn terminal from Burton-in-Kendal.

41. Hanging bowl mount from the Arnside area (LVPL1646)

AD 800–900

Length: 30 mm; Width: 15 mm

Eighth-century Irish vessel mount. The copper-alloy mount is dominated by a grim human face, with large oval eyes, above panels of enamel. It was originally symmetrical, with a matching face in mirror image at the bottom. It would have been made as one of a set of three rim-mounts for a bowl of thin copper-alloy sheet. These mounts were recessed behind to hold rings from which the bowl could be hung. The Arnside mount has three holes drilled through it, including a large one through the mouth, showing that the mount has been reattached or reused.

The stylised staring face and the lavish use of enamel are features characteristic of eighth-century Irish decorative metalwork. Similar anthropomorphic mounts have also been found on Irish bowls and buckets in Norway. Irish mounts and fittings also travelled with the Vikings as loot or traded goods, or possibly as gifts and dowry pieces. While often of no value as bullion, they were appreciated for their decoration, bright gilding and coloured enamel. Many, as here, show signs of reuse.

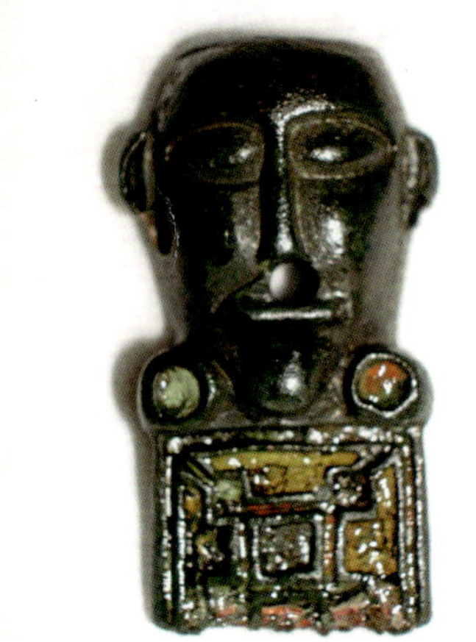

LVPL1646: Hanging bowl mount from the Arnside area.

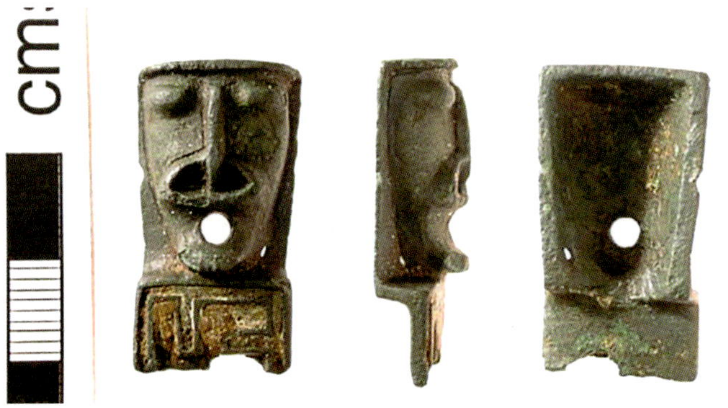

LVPL-5D64F3: Hanging bowl mount from Husthwaite, North Yorkshire.

Chapter 6
Medieval

In the eleventh century, the Normans took over the rule of Cumbria: in 1066, they took the southern district, which includes the baronies of Millom, Furness, Kendale and Lonsdale, and in 1092, the northern district (Carlisle and surrounding territories) was taken by William Rufus.

After William had reclaimed Cumbria, the county's economy and the number of markets, charters, settlements and population grew well into the later twelfth and early thirteenth centuries. This also includes religious sites such as Furness Abbey, which was founded in 1123 and gradually enlarged and rebuilt by the Cistercians throughout the twelfth century.

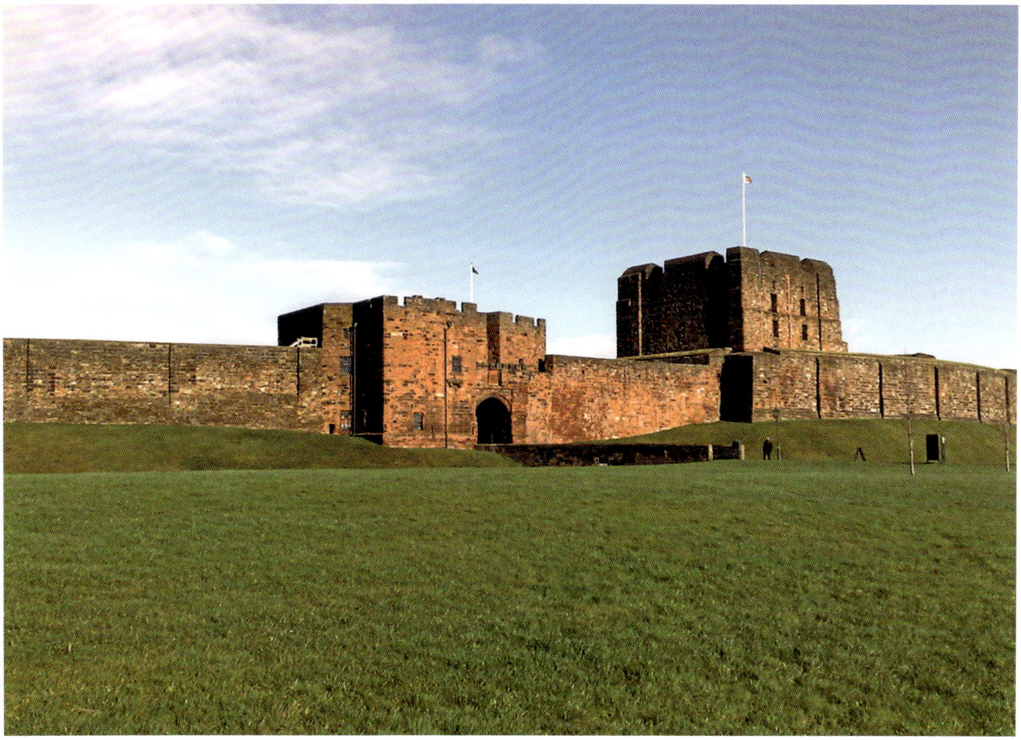

Carlisle Castle. (Neil Boothman, via Wikimedia Commons)

By the fifteenth century, it had grown into the second-richest and most powerful Cistercian abbey in England. The monks of the abbey were also landowners, and the most powerful body in what was then a remote border territory. Cumbria was – and still is – a very rural country, and trade was dominantly local, but there would have been strong connections – spiritual and economical – across the Irish Sea to Man and Ireland, and Scotland and Northern England. Local towns such as Kendal and Penrith were centres for local trade, especially wool and related products, while the wider trade network probably only incorporated Carlisle. However, as a city situated in the border region between England and Scotland, Carlisle saw a number of invasions and raids between the late thirteenth century and the unifications of the crowns in 1603.

The fourteenth century was especially hard for the people in north Cumbria and Carlisle, with Scottish invasions in 1315 and 1322, and raids in the 1330s and 1340s. In addition, Cumbria was plagued by famine, the plague and animal murrain of cattle and sheep, which had a devastating effect on local economies.

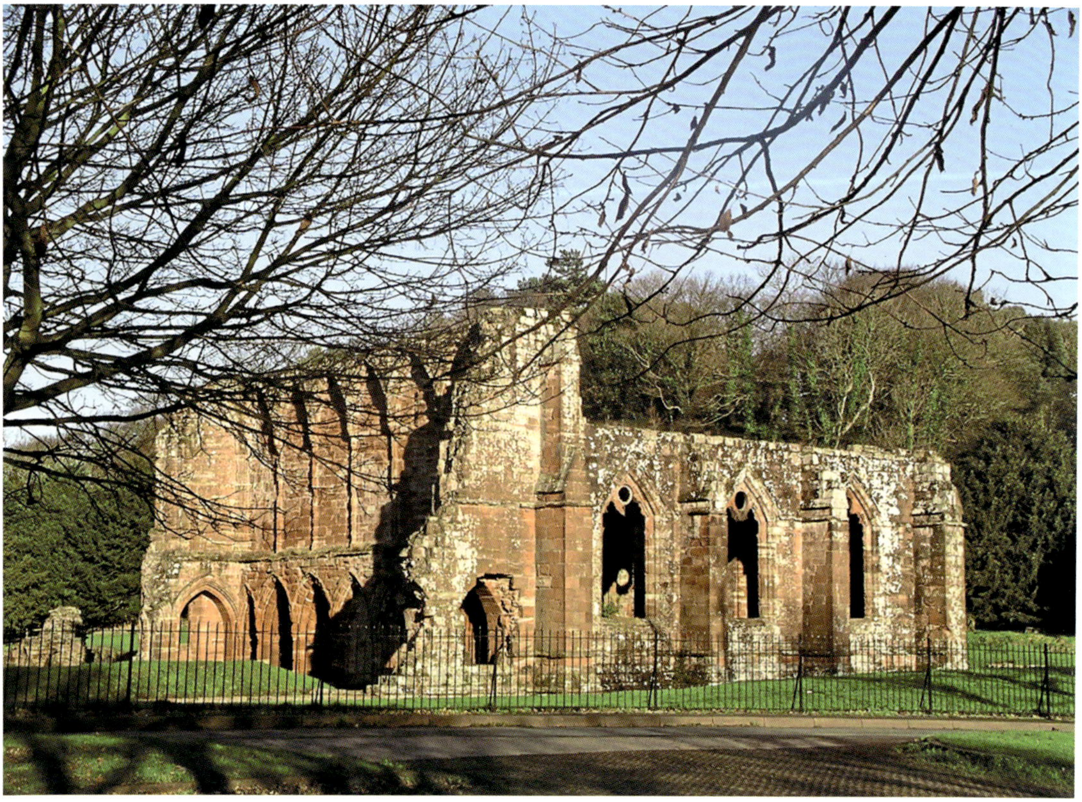

Furness Abbey. (MikeF, via Wikimedia Commons)

42. George and Dragon badge from the Orton area (LANCUM-4501B2)
Fifteenth-century.
The length of the George is 40 mm, width 9 mm, thickness 5 mm and weight is 8.43 g. The length of the dragon is 30 mm, width 15 mm, thickness 4 mm and weight 6.33 g.

Medieval silver gilt cap or hat badge of St George slaying the dragon. The two figures were originally soldered together (although probably cast in two pieces), and the saint also has a small attachment hook soldered to his back. He is depicted raising his sword over the dragon, who is cowering at his feet, looking up, tail curled around his hind legs. The saint wears armour with articulated elbow and knee pieces, but no helmet. His face, hair and the dragon's anxious expression are finely moulded.

The cult of St George was closely associated with the Chapel of St George, Windsor, which was built by Edward IV (reigned 1461–70, and 1471–83) and Henry VII (reigned 1485–1509). Pilgrimage to the chapel, where relics including the saint's heart and leg were kept, reached a peak in the period spanning the late fifteenth to mid-sixteenth centuries. It is likely that this badge dates from the same period.

There are several other examples on the database, the two closest from Appleby (Cumbria, LANCUM-619B37) and Milton-under-Wychwood (Oxfordshire, BH-D9F03F).

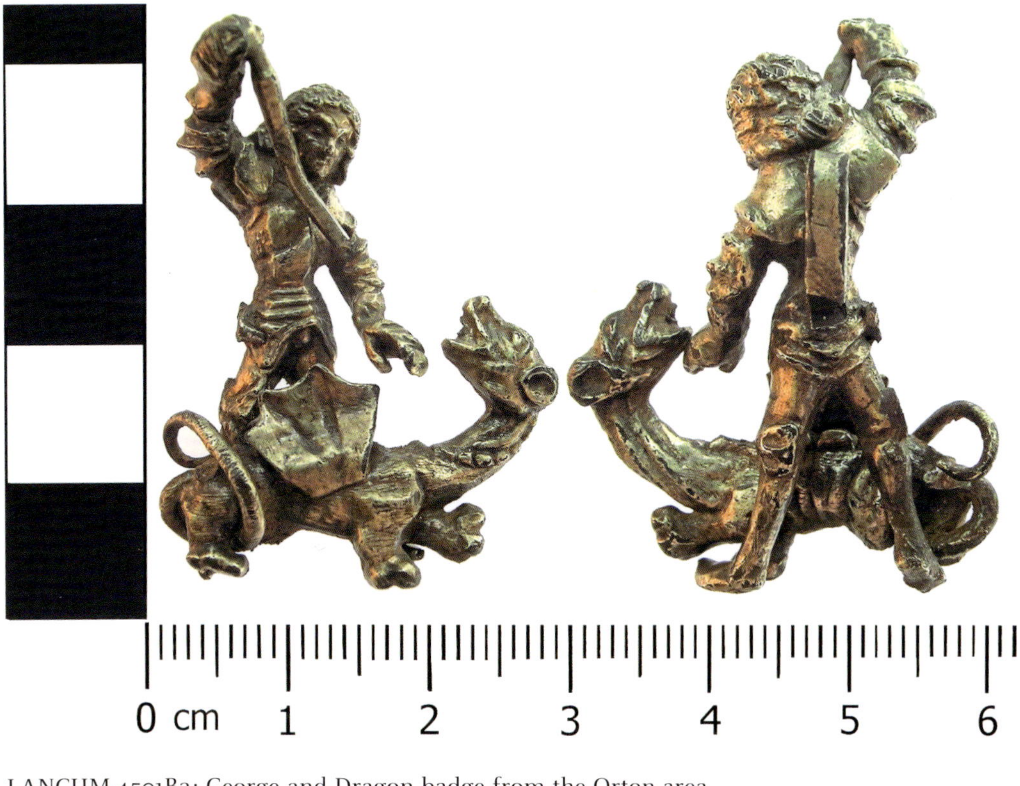

LANCUM-4501B2: George and Dragon badge from the Orton area.

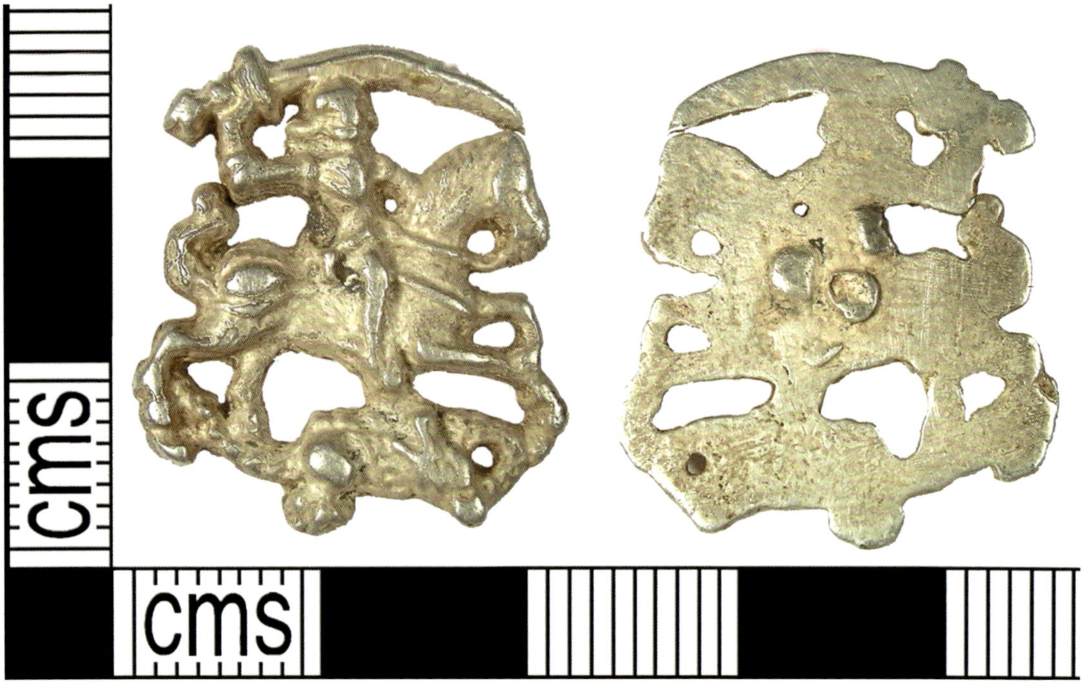

LANCUM-619B37: George and Dragon badge from Appleby, Cumbria.

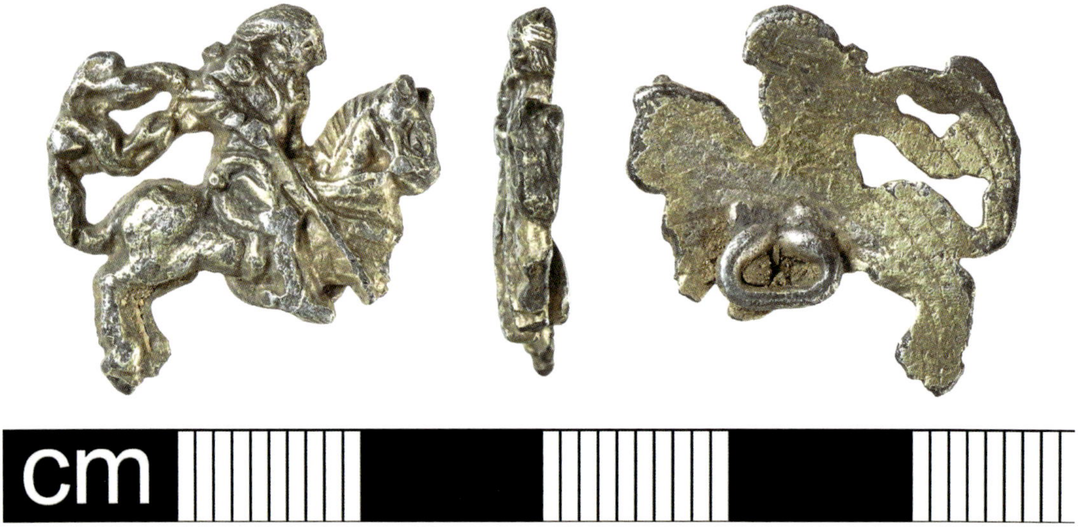

BH-D9F03F: George and Dragon badge from Milton-under-Wychwood, Oxfordshire.

43. Penny of Prince Henry, Early of Northumberland from Maulds Meaburn (LANCUM-C7BD67)

AD 1139–1152
Thickness: 0.5 mm; Weight: 1.54 g; Diameter: 20 mm

Medieval silver hammered penny of Prince Henry, Earl of Northumberland and Huntingdon, dating from *c.* AD 1139–1152. David I got involved in the English Civil War because of Matilda (or Maud) and, in 1138, David I's forces were soundly defeated at the battle of Cowton Moor, near Northallerton, by an alliance of northern English barons. Despite this defeat, he continued to resist the forces of the English ruler Stephen; Stephen, having been worn down from fighting a two-front war, agreed to sign a treaty with David I, recognising David I's claims to Northumberland. This earldom was shortly thereafter bestowed on his second son, Prince Henry, who was the heir to the Scottish throne. Prince Henry would continue to hold this earldom throughout the rest of his lifetime. His death in 1152 would catapult his son, Malcolm, into being the heir of the throne of Scotland on the death of his grandfather, David I, in 1154. This earldom had the benefit of its mints at Carlisle, Corbridge and possibly Bamburgh.

This coinage of pennies being struck in Henry's name had the legend 'HENRICVS COM' or 'N ENCI CON' (i.e., 'Henry, Count').

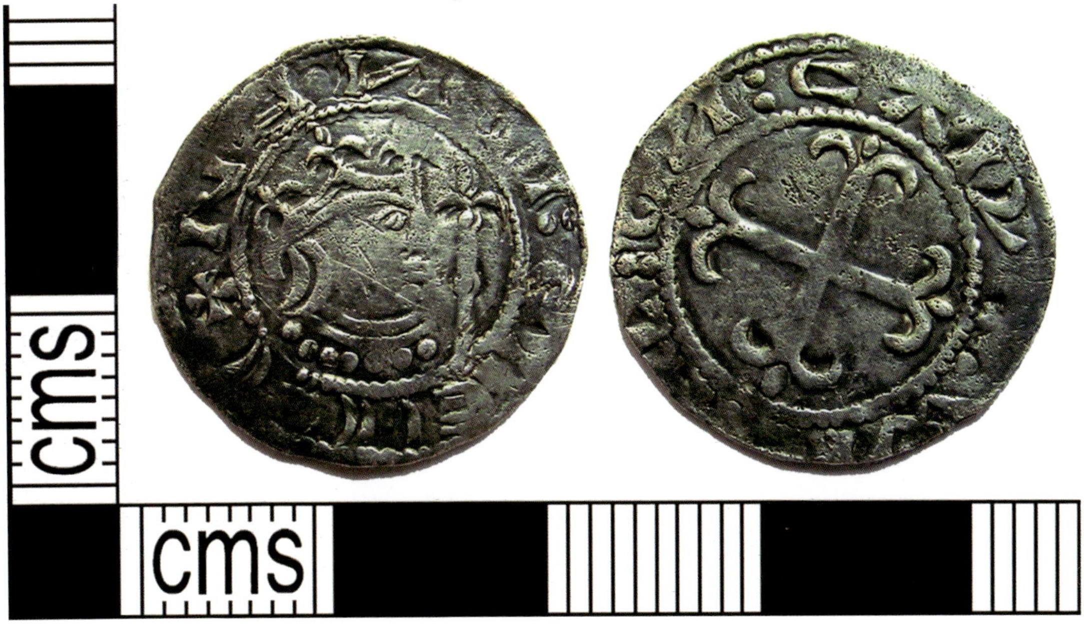

LANCUM-C7BD67: Penny of Prince Henry, Earl of Northumberland, from Maulds Meaburn.

44. Medieval mount from the Kendal area (LANCUM-F95DC6)

Fourteenth- to sixteenth-century AD

Length: 34.5 mm; Width: 29 mm; Thickness: 2 mm; Weight: 11.83 g

Cast copper-alloy box or casket mount, dating from the fourteenth to sixteenth centuries AD. The mount retains some gilding on the obverse in the grooves of the design. It has a short projection on the reverse for attachment to an object; it is suggested here that, even though it could also be a decorative book mount, the projection is too long for the cover of a leather-bound book. It is more likely that the mount was attached to a box or casket. It displays a winged lion with an almost human-like face, which probably means that this is a depiction of the evangelist St Mark. It could be envisioned that this mount was one of a set of four (the others being a man, a bull and an eagle for St Luke, St Matthew and St John) that adorned the four corners of the casket's or box's lid, possibly a reliquary.

A very similar one was recorded from Bolton Percy (North Yorkshire, LVPL-F667A7).

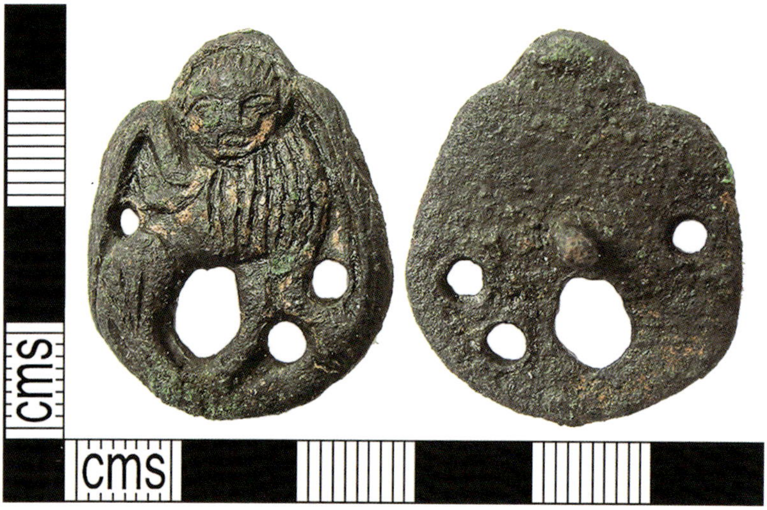

LANCUM-F95DC6: Medieval mount from the Kendal area.

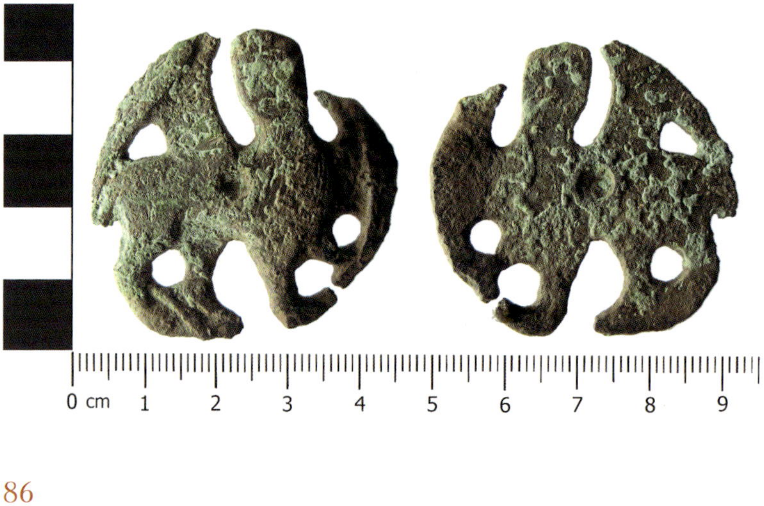

LVPL-F667A7: Medieval mount from Bolton Percy, North Yorkshire.

Chapter 7
Post-Medieval and Modern

The sixteenth century was very difficult for Cumbria, mainly because of its geographical location between England and Scotland. The Tudor period was one of political turmoil in the region: the sixteenth century was marked both by the continuing and increasing attacks of the Border Reivers (local clans fighting for land and overlordship) in the north and west of the county, and by the religious reformation initiated and overseen by Henry VIII, which resulted in the dissolution of important Cumbrian ecclesiastical sites such as Furness Abbey and Lanercost Priory.

In the 300 years leading up to the union of the English and Scottish crowns in 1603, Cumbria suffered much as a border county from military clashes between England and Scotland, as well as from the constant fighting of the Borderland clans – the Border Reivers. The Border Reivers were characterised by strong kinship bonds, forming clan-like groups under a given surname. These groups became semiautonomous from local government, owing far more loyalty to their name than to the king or local lords.

The Reivers take their name from the fact that they lived by raiding (from the Old English *rēafian*, 'to rob'), rustling cattle and sheep from across the border, and even looting the armies of their own king, such was their antipathy towards their nations.

In 1566 James Hepburn (1534–1578), the fourth Earl of Bothwell, was appointed as Lord Warden of the Scottish Marches. He was determined to subdue the Border Reivers, especially the most prominent Reiver, who went by the name of Jock Elliot. However, the ballad of Jock Elliott tells us how Jock overpowered Bothwell and how, upon return to his castle, Bothwell, badly shaken and with severe wounds to his head, found that it had been taken by the Reivers. The raids stopped only when the border effectively lost its meaning after the Union in 1603.

Modern Cumbria is renowned for a few, important industries, such as shipbuilding (Vickers Shipbuilding Engineering Limited in Barrow-in-Furness) and the ironworks at Seaton and Barrow's Hematite Steel Company. More than industry, however, Cumbria is known as the county of the 'Lake District', which became a well-known and much-loved destination for travellers, mountaineers and explorers in the eighteenth and nineteenth centuries.

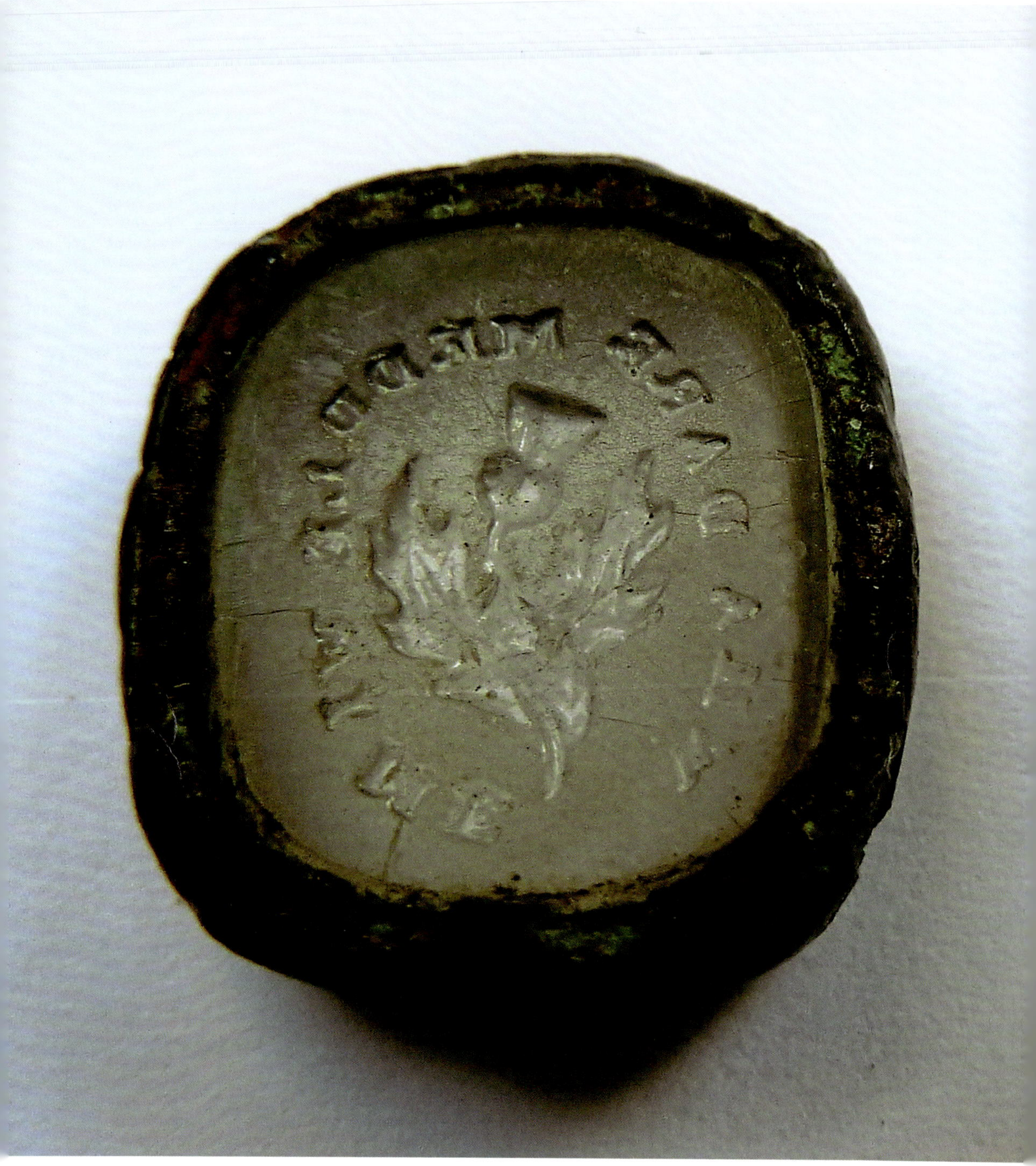

LANCUM-9E6B02: Reiver's seal matrix from Ince Blundell, Sefton. The inscription around the thistle reads: *Wha daur meddle wi me,* which is the first line of the ballad of Jock Elliot. (Brian Rendall)

45. Vessel for keeping lead weights (LANCUM-90DB4D)

Sixteenth- to seventeenth-century
Height: 22 mm; Weight: 45.9 g; Diameter: 34 mm

A complete circular hinged copper-alloy container for a set of (possibly three) nested cup weights, dating from the post-medieval period, most likely from the sixteenth or seventeenth century. The vessel is very good condition, with a smooth green patina on the outside and a slightly rougher, brownish colour on the inside. The example from Cumbria has official stamps on the lid: a crown and what looks like a key or an anchor. A complete example was recorded from North Yorkshire (SWYOR-2F0735).

The container from North Yorkshire contained a nest of three cup weights of different sizes. The first has a mass of 30.72 g, which is 1.08 ounces and would have been used as a 1 ounce weight. The other two weights were fused together. They have a combined mass of 23 g (0.8 ounces) and would have been half-ounce and quarter-ounce weights. The sets from Cumbria and North Yorkshire may have also included a quarter-ounce flat weight, which would have fitted inside the smallest cup.

This style of lid, with reinforcing struts, is characteristic of a post-medieval date and, perhaps, manufacture in the major centre of Nuremberg. Precise dating is difficult as cup weights were used from the fifteenth to the nineteenth centuries (Biggs, 1995, Bullion Weights, page 16), but a sixteenth- or seventeenth-century date is most likely.

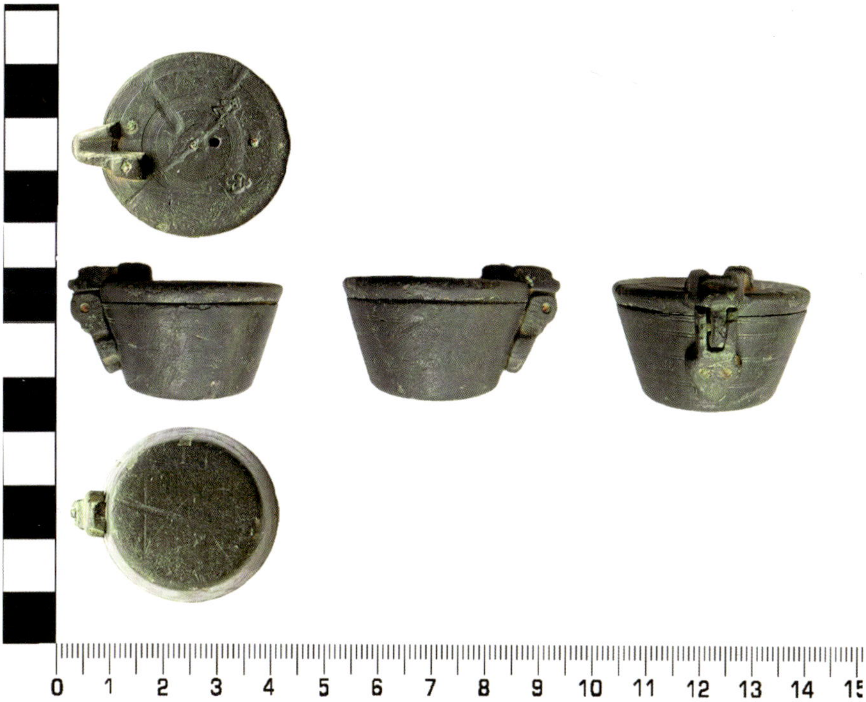

ANCUM-90DB4D: Vessel for keeping nested cup weights from the Brampton area.

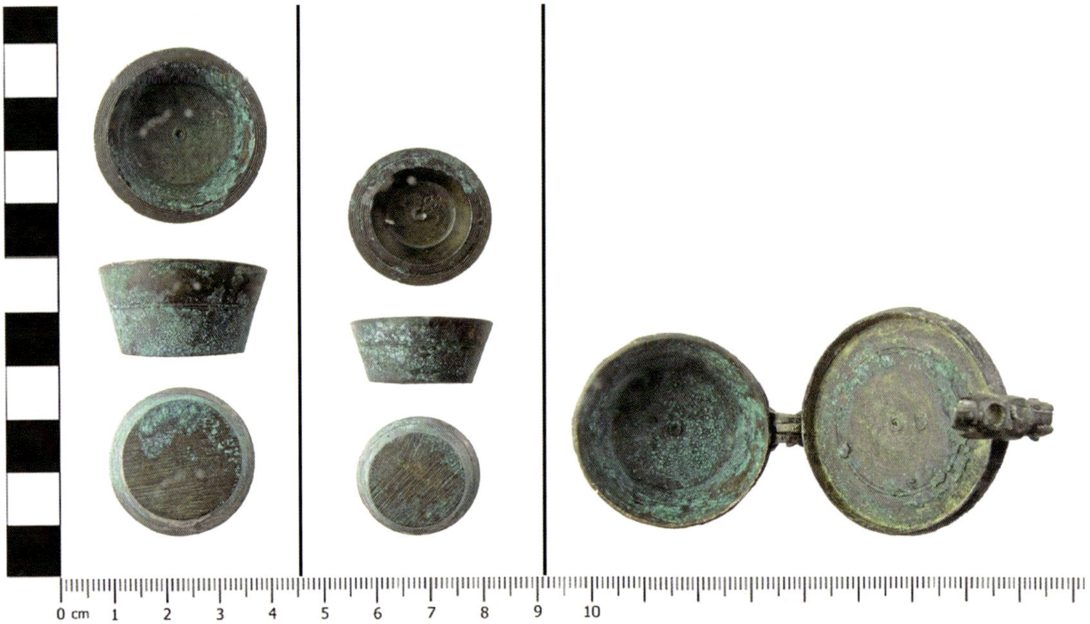

Above and below: SWYOR-2F0735: Vessel for keeping nested cup weights from Burton Leonard, North Yorkshire.

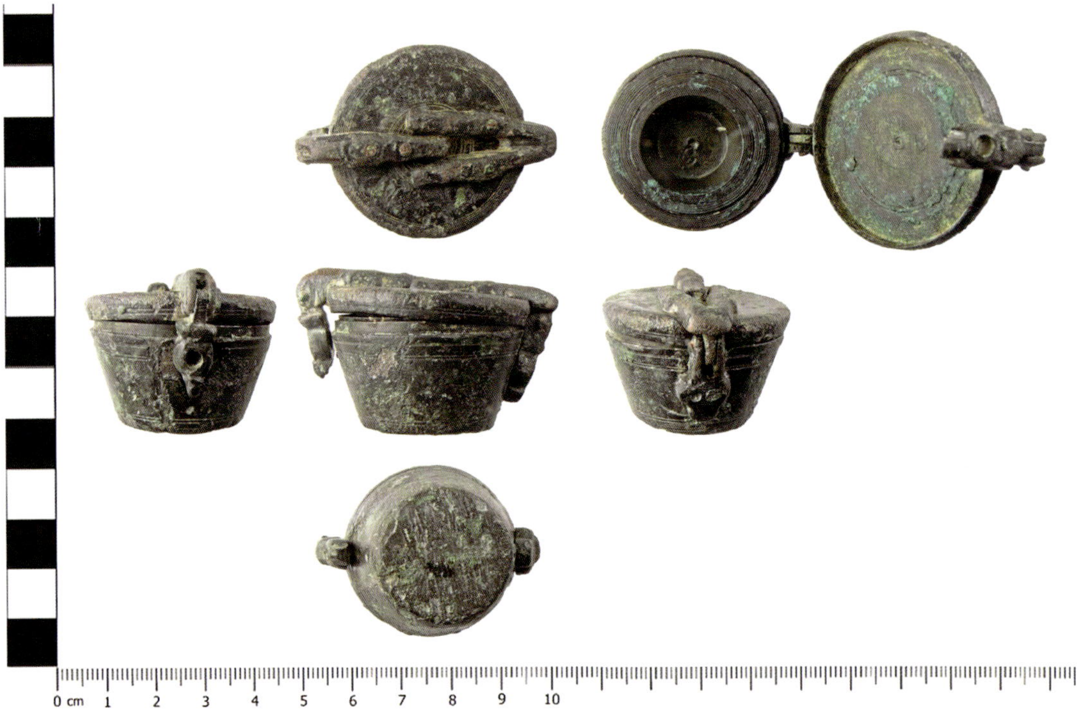

46. Complete gunflint from the Mawbray area: LANCUM-FF9BA4
Seventeenth- to eighteenth-century
Length: 24 mm; Width: 21.5 mm, Thickness: 10.5 mm, Weight: 15.05 g

A late post-medieval to early modern gunflint from a flint-lock rifle or musket, dating to the seventeenth to eighteenth centuries. The gunflint is still in its lead case/holder. The gunflint is sub-square in plan and appears complete. The flint has been knapped around the edges in order to get the correct shape. The distal edge is thinner and the flint is triangular in section. All of the edges are relatively straight. The flint used is a dark-brown to black colour. The lead case is still complete, encasing about 40 to 50 per cent of the flint. It seems to have been made from a long piece of lead, one side rounded, the other straight, with an oval perforation in the centre, which was presumably part of the suspension mechanism.

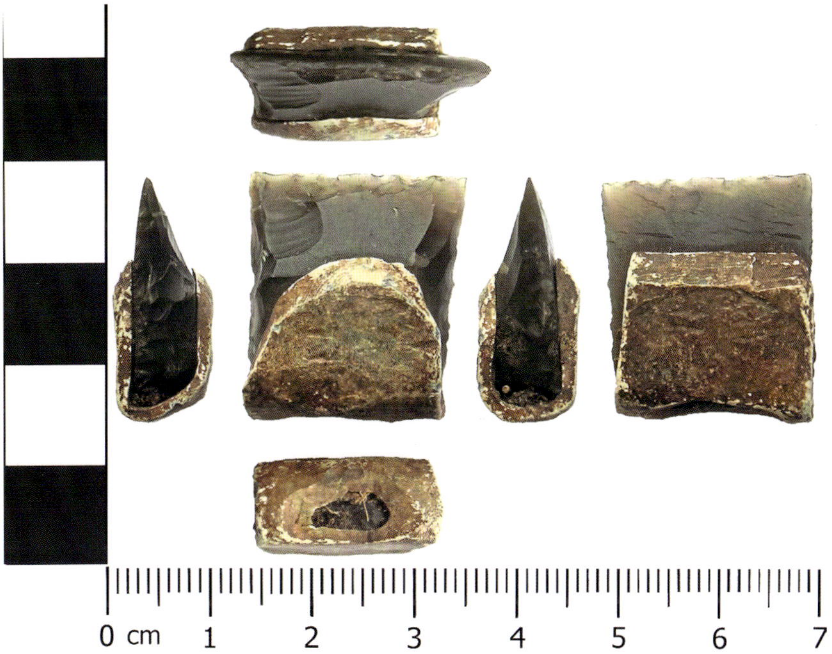

LANCUM-FF9BA4: Complete gunflint from the Mawbray area.

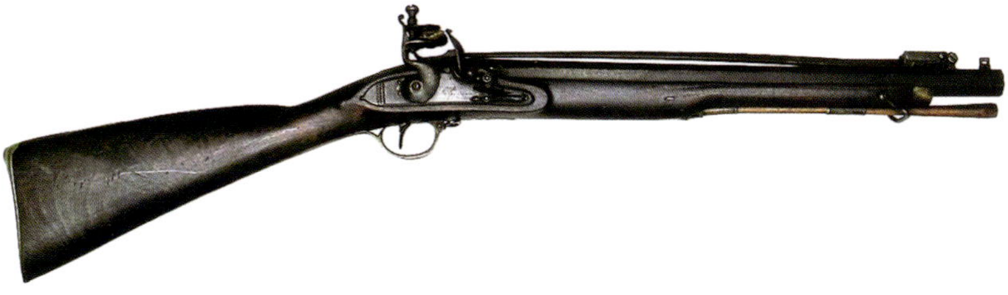

Flintlock gun dating from the mid-eighteenth century.
(Adam's Guns; www.adamsguns.com)

47. Chinese coin hoard from the Barrow-in-Furness area: LANCUM-0095B8

1659–1850

In 2011, a metal detectorist discovered a large coin hoard of 108 Chinese coins near Dalton-in-Furness. Barrow-in-Furness has to this day a thriving Chinese community, members of which are the descendants of the first Chinese shipbuilders, who came over in the nineteenth century to work in Barrow's docks. Qin Cao, a trainee curator for Asian coins at the British Museum at the time, wrote the Treasure Report for this unusual find.

The 107 coins and one fragment are all cast copper-alloy pieces with square holes in the middle, and are 'cash coins' of East Asia. The coins were reported to have been found tied together with a thread. In East Asia, it was customary to pass a thread through the central hole to create a 'string of coins', but the thread fell apart in this case as the coins were being lifted out of the ground. Some remains of the thread were collected and preserved in two plastic bags. The coins are all of the same denomination: 1-cash. 104 coins are from the Chinese Qing dynasty (1644–1911), ranging in date from 1659 to 1850. The earliest coin, of which there is only one example, has the inscription 'Shunzhi tongbao' and was cast between 1659 and 1661 at the Yunnan mint. The majority of the Qing coins (fifty-six) were produced during the Daoguang reign period (1821–1850) at a variety of mints in China. Two coins are Vietnamese coins issued during the Canh Hung reign period (1740–1786) of the Restored Le dynasty (1592–1789) and the Canh Thinh reign period (1793–1802) of the Tay Son dynasty (1778–1802), respectively. Two groups comprising three and two coins were found corroded together. The coins on top of both of these corroded groups are Daoguang tongbao. The rest are illegible, along with one coin and a fragment from the main hoard.

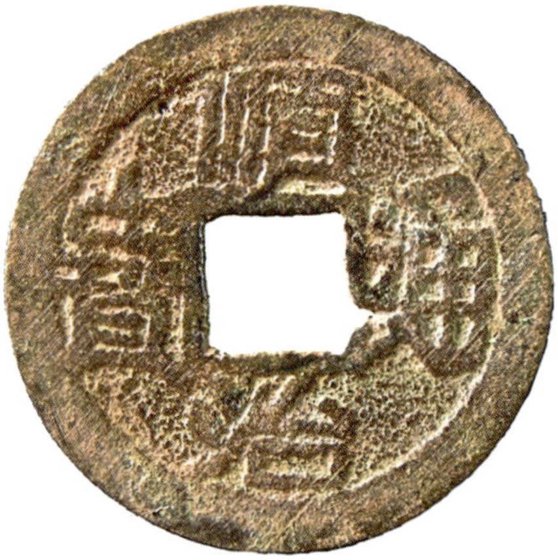

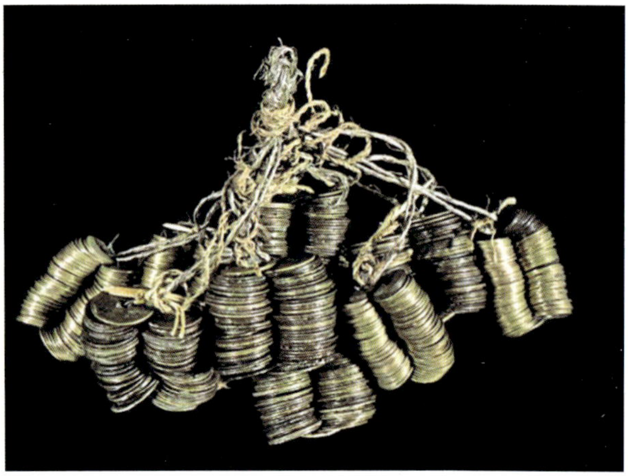

Above left: LANCUM-0095B8: One cash coin from the Chinese coin hoard from the Barrow-in-Furness area.

Above right: Seventeenth- to nineteenth-century Chinese cash coins tied together with string. (Qin Cao)

48. Three countermarked cartwheel pennies from Borrowdale (LANCUM-7A3022)
1820s/1830s

Three early modern tokens dating from the early nineteenth century. They are three cartwheel pennies, which were found in a wall at Borrowdale. All three were polished and countermarked with sun-shaped stamps, and were possibly turned into tokens for wall labourers.

The British cartwheel penny and twopence was made in 1797 and 1798 because King George III wanted the British population to possess a coin that was equal in value to the actual value of copper at that time. However, the coins turned out to be extremely unpopular with the general population because of their monstrous weight and size. The other reason is that this coin suffered considerable damage because of its size. It was too cumbersome to carry around a lot of large and heavy loose change in the purse or pouch for average everyday purchases. So the term 'cartwheel' was given to these coins because people complained they were as big as cartwheels.

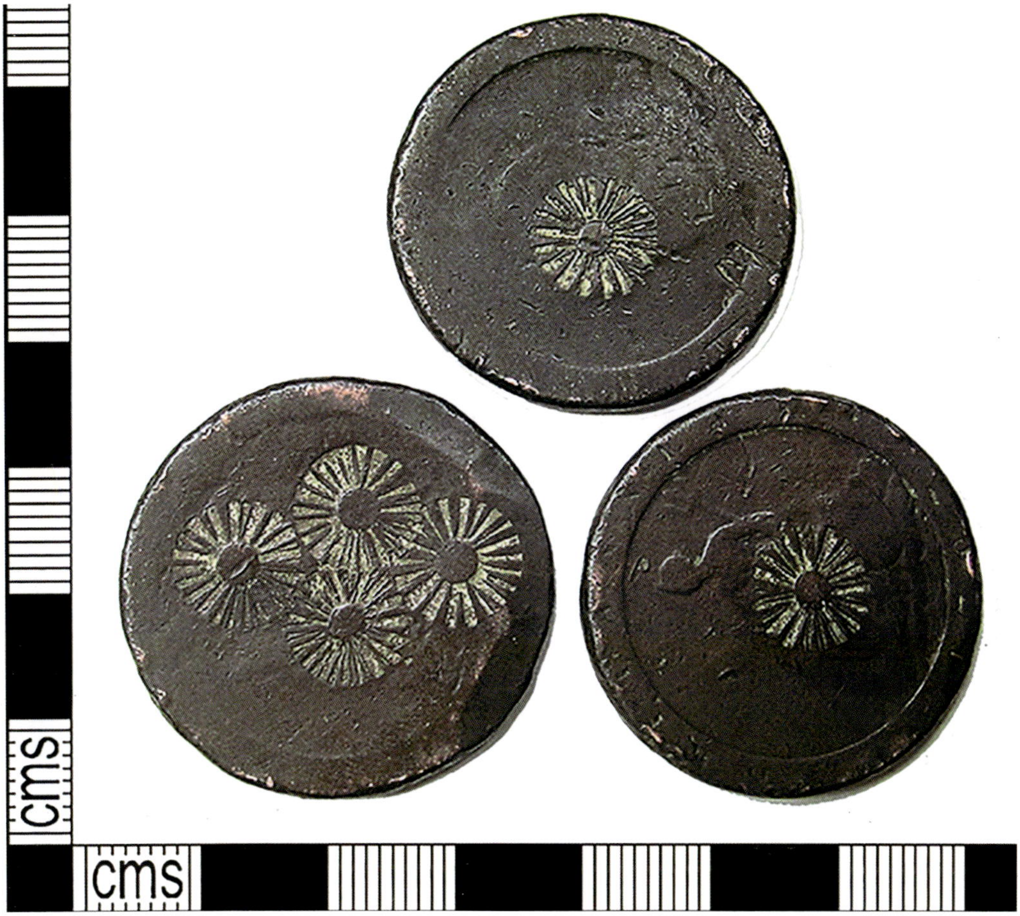

LANCUM-7A3022: Three countermarked cartwheel pennies from Borrowdale.

49. Spoon mould from the Windermere area (LANCUM-EDCD76)
Eighteenth- to nineteenth-century
Length: 240 mm; Width: 55 mm; Thickness: 41 mm

Two halves of a copper-alloy spoon mould for casting large pewter table spoons. There are no defining features on the end product, such as a rat's tail or shell decoration; the end product would have been quite plain. However, spoon moulds such as this are rare finds, and this is the only one recorded on the database. It is complete and could still be used today.

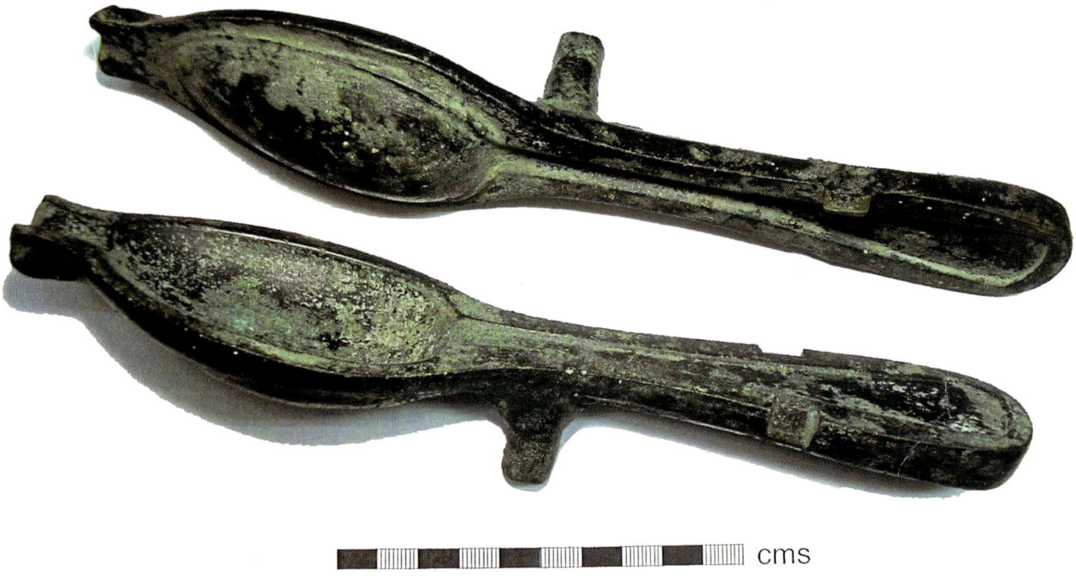

LANCUM-EDCD76: Spoon mould from the Windermere area.

50. Gold dentures from the Arnside area (LANCUM-3DE363)
1838–1920
Length: 67.9 mm; Width: 41.1 mm; Thickness: 10 mm; Weight: 28.55 g

Gold dentures dating from the later nineteenth century or early twentieth century. The base is made of gold but the teeth themselves are porcelain. The gold would have been 'swaged', which means that a wax impression was taken of the patient's mouth and, from this, a plaster model was made. A further metal or lead model was then shaped, and the sheet of gold was placed on top and hammered with a horn mallet. Swaging is a technique used very occasionally today but, in general, had died out by the mid-twentieth century. Porcelain tube teeth, such as the ones on this denture, were developed by Claudius Ash in 1838. Initially the teeth were made, then a hole was reamed into them and a gold tube was inserted. This was then placed on the post, which had been soldered to the gold plate. Later on, platinum tubes were developed and the porcelain teeth could be fired with the platinum tube already inside.

Gold dentures are frequently found by metal detectorists and, although not very old, they rank among the oddest finds from pasture and ploughed land.

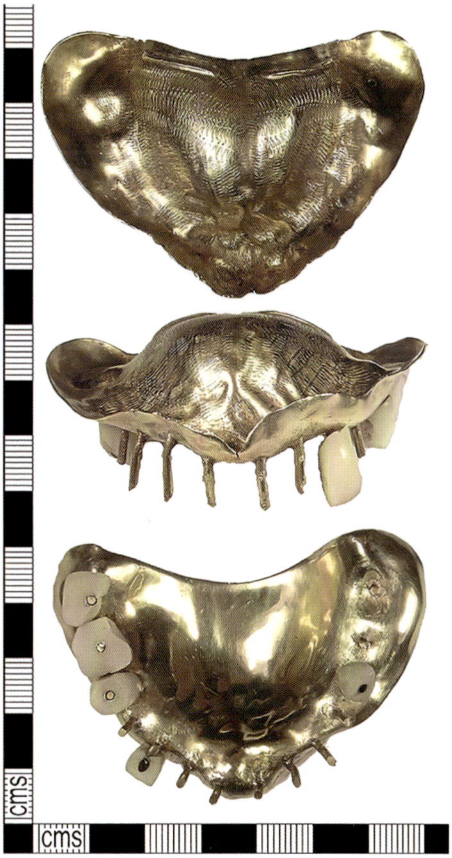

LANCUM-3DE363: Gold dentures from the Arnside area.

Bibliography

Breeze, D. (ed.), *The First Souvenirs: Enamelled Vessels from Hadrian's Wall* (Cumberland: Cumberland and Westmorland Antiquarian and Archaeological Society, 2012).

Brennand, M. (ed.), 'The Archaeology of North West England: An Archaeological Research Framework for North West England: Volume I, Resource Assessment', *Archaeology North West*, 8 (2006).

Brooks, C., Daniels, R. and Harding, A. (editors), 'Past, Present and Future, the Archaeology of Northern England: Proceedings of a Conference held in Durham in 1996', *Architectural and Archaeological Society of Durham and Northumberland Research Report*, 5 (2002).

Evans, H., 'Neolithic and Bronze Age Landscapes of Cumbria', *British Archaeological Reports (British Series)*, 463 (2008).

Griffiths, D., *Vikings of the Irish Sea* (Stroud: The History Press, 2010).

McMarthy, M. R. (ed.), *Roman and Medieval Carlisle: The Southern Lanes.* (Carlisle: Carlisle Archaeology Ltd, 2000).

Paterson, C., Parsons. A., Newman, R., Johnson, N. and Howard Davis, C., *Shadows in the Sands. Excavation of a Viking-Age Cemetery at Cumwhitton, Cumbria* (Oxford: Oxford Archaeology North, 2014).

Saunders, T. (ed.), *Hillforts in the North West and Beyond.* (Council for British Archaeology North West, 2014).

Shotter, D., *Romans and Britons in North-West England* (Lancaster: Centre for North West Regional Studies, University of Lancaster, 2004).

Shotter, D., *Roman Coins from North West England.* (Lancaster: Centre for North West Regional Studies, University of Lancaster, 2011).

Shotter, D., 'Two hoards of denarii from north-west Cumbria', *Transactions of the Cumberland & Westmorland Antiquarian & Archaeological Society*, 15 (2015), 221–229.